Gothick
ΠΟRTHΛΜPTΟΠSHIRE

Jack Gould

Shire Publications Ltd

Contents

Printed in Great Britain by C. I. Thomas & Sons (Haverfordwest) Ltd, Press Buildings, Merlins Bridge, Haverfordwest, Dyfed SA61 1XF.

British Library Cataloguing in Publication Data: Gould, Jack. Gothick Northamptonshire. — (Gothick Guides; No. 4). I. Title. II. Series. 914.25504. ISBN 0-7478-0185-1.

Series Editor: Jennifer Westwood

Acknowledgements

The author gratefully acknowledges the help given in compiling this book by the writings of Marian Pipe, Alan Burman, C. E. Eastwood (the Rouse murder), B. E. Hensman (Scaldwell) and the numerous ladies whose joint contributions in the Women's Institutes *Village Book* led to many corners of the county.

The late Victor Hatley, George Freeston, Marian Arnold and staff of the Local History Room at the Abington Street Library, Northampton, and Trevor Cooper, Librarian of the *Chronicle and Echo* newspaper, have also afforded essential assistance.

The photographs are acknowledged as follows: Compton Estates, page 15; Mary Gould, pages 7 (top),8, 12 (bottom), 13, 18 (top), 37, 38, 39 (both), 40, 44, 56 and 59 (bottom); Cadbury Lamb, pages 10 (bottom), 12 (top), 14 (bottom), 19, 21, 22 (both), 33, 34 (left), 35 (bottom), 43, 45, 46, 53, 54 (bottom), 57 (both), 58, 60, 62 (both) and 63; Northampton Mercury Company Ltd, pages 5 (bottom), 10-11 (top), 24, 28, 30, 32 (top), 35 (top), 41 (Roland Holloway Collection), 42, 48, 49, 50, 52 (Alan Burman Collection) and 54 (top); Marian Pipe, pages 11 (bottom), 25, 53 and 59 (top).

The line drawings are by Rachel Lewis, except that on page 32 which is by Edward Stamp and the battle plan on page 36 which is by Shirley Barker; the map on page 4 is by Robert Dizon. The cover design is based on a painting by Michael J. Taylor entitled 'Overgrown Lodge'.

Using this book

The numbers preceding the directions at the end of each entry are sheet numbers and grid references for Ordnance Survey Landranger maps. Opening times of houses and gardens mentioned as being open to the public can be found in *Historic Houses, Castles and Gardens Open to the Public* (British Leisure Publications, published annually).

Introduction

Northamptonshire may appear to be an unspectacular tract of middle England but it has myths and legends rivalling those of the Celtic west. It has even been suggested that *Bannaventa*, the Roman station on the Watling Street near Daventry, was the home of St Patrick before he was forcibly removed to Ireland. St Rumbold (Rumwold) at King's Sutton and St Werburga at Weedon Bec have left legends as strange as any and Northampton has its own martyred St Ragener emerging from the Dark Ages.

Wherever woodland abounds there is likely to be the tradition of the spectral huntsman. In Germany he was known as the *Wilde Jäger* and travellers in Windsor Forest dreaded an encounter with Herne the Hunter, since these apparitions were accompanied by a 'goblin pack', the sight and sound of which in full cry were truly fearsome.

In medieval times great tracts of England came under the Forest Laws. These were designed to protect the King's deer (as hunting in those areas was a royal prerogative) and the woodland that provided their habitat. At that time there was talk of 'the Forest between the two bridges', meaning those at Oxford and Stamford, and including the royal forests of Whittlewood, Salcey and Rockingham — so that there was woodland throughout most of the length of the county of Northamptonshire. The Anglo-Saxon Chronicle of 1127 recorded that a 'Wild Hunt' galloped through the deer park of Peterborough and the woods up to Stamford, the Soke of Peterborough then being reckoned a part of Northamptonshire. The tradition was also attached to Whittlebury Forest, or Whittlewood (see Towcester). In this case the ghostly hounds were in pursuit of the wraith of a young woman.

Two old sayings suggest turpitude on the part of the inhabitants of certain places:

Brackley breed, better to hang than feed.

This jesting slander emanated from Evenley when the nearby market town fell on hard times and 'unprofitable members of the commonwealth' abounded there. The other condemned:

Great Houghton, wicked people,
Sold their bells to build a steeple.

In 1754 the old church tower with five bells was replaced by the present spire.

Real wickedness was abroad in the 1780s at Culworth, from where a gang of villains terrorised the surrounding countryside. The most colourful member was William Abbott, who was the parish clerk at neighbouring Sulgrave and, according to an account written only fifty years after his being sentenced to transportation to Australia, 'always carried pistols about his person, even when fulfilling the sacred duties of his office'. Some of the loot from the robberies was stored in the parish chest at Sulgrave.

The river Nene flows through most of the county and disastrous floods have occurred. Before modern drainage heavy rain in the upper reaches could cause flash floods lower down the course of the river. When Wansford was in the Soke of Peterborough and so deemed part of Northamptonshire a rustic full of ale went to sleep on a haycock in a waterside meadow. Later he awoke to find himself borne along on a great torrent of flood water. As he passed a house where the dwellers had taken refuge in an upper storey they called out to him, asking where he came from. Lost and bewildered, he bellowed in reply 'Wansford in England!' and this became a common catchphrase.

The following epitaph existed in Ecton churchyard until the stone weathered and it became illegible:

Here snug in grave my wife do lie,
Now she's at rest and so am I.

Another husband who did not love

3

Introduction

his wife wholeheartedly was John Harvey Thursby, an eighteenth-century member of the family of squires at Abington, now a part of Northampton. The inscription on Mrs Thursby's memorial in the church of St Peter and St Paul ends with the equivocal judgment: 'What sort of Woman she was the last Day will determine.'

Gothick
NORTHAMPTONSHIRE

Places mentioned in the gazetteer

LINCOLNSHIRE

LEICESTERSHIRE

WARWICKSHIRE

CAMBRIDGESHIRE

BEDFORDSHIRE

BUCKINGHAMSHIRE

OXFORDSHIRE

Easton on the Hill
Apethorpe
Bulwick
Deene
Fotheringhay
Rockingham Forest
Rockingham
Weldon
Cotterstock
Corby
Oundle
Wilbarston
Stanion
Newton in the Willows
Brigstock
Geddington
Barnwell
Rushton
Barford Bridge
Boughton House
Sudborough
Rothwell
Harrington
Weekley
Twywell
Clopton
Naseby
Woodford
Stanford on Avon
Lamport
Faxton
Burton Latimer
Ringstead
Guilsborough
Crick
Scaldwell
Orlingbury
Raunds
Kilsby
Brixworth
Hannington
Great Harrowden
Hargrave
Ashby St Ledgers
Pitsford
Sywell
Wellingborough
Braunston
Welton
Great Brington
Boughton
Mears Ashby
Wilby
Whilton
Daventry
Northampton
Litte Houghton
Grendon
Weedon Bec
Nether Heyford
Castle Ashby
Easton Maudit
Stowe Nine Churches
Hardingstone
Yardley Hastings
Charwelton
Pattishall
Gayton
Eastcote
Blisworth
Salcey Forest
Towcester
Culworth
Lois Weedon
Grafton Regis
Heathencote
Wappenham
Paulerspury
Silverstone
Whittlebury
Syresham
Cosgrove
Puxley
Deanshanger
Passenham
King's Sutton

0   5   10 Miles
0   5   10   15 Kilometres

4

A gazetteer of Gothick places

Apethorpe

This peaceful place is said to be haunted by an uncommon phenomenon, a happy ghost. In 1621 the Mildmay Chapel, thought by Pevsner to be among the best of its date in England, was added to the parish church of St Leonard to house the huge monument to Sir Anthony Mildmay and his wife, she having died the previous year. Lady Grace Mildmay has sometimes been seen gliding silently through Apethorpe Hall, scattering silver pennies as she goes. She was, according to her epitaph, 'compassionate in heart and charitably helpful with physic, clothes, nourishment, or counsels to any in misery'.

OS 141: TL 023957. Apethorpe is on a by-road 7 miles (11 km) north of Oundle. A hump-backed bridge over the Willow Brook leads to the church. The hall is not open to the public but can be seen from the road from Apethorpe to Woodnewton.

The gatehouse at Ashby St Ledgers, where the Gunpowder Plot was reputedly planned.

Ashby St Ledgers

Sir William Catesby, lord of the manor here at the time of Richard III, was the second of the three royal favourites lampooned in the memorable couplet:

> The Rat, the Cat and Lovell our Dog
> Rule all England under the Hog.

The Rat was Sir Richard Ratcliffe; the badge of Lord Lovell of Titchmarsh, also in the county, was topped by the figure of a dog and the king's insignia was that of a charging boar. Collingbourn, who wrote the verse, was hanged, drawn and quartered on Tower Hill and Sir William was beheaded at Leicester three days after the defeat at Bosworth Field in 1485.

His descendant Robert Catesby led the conspiracy of the Gunpowder Plot when he lived at Lapworth in Warwickshire but a strong tradition holds that the gatehouse at Ashby was a meeting place of the plotters. Certainly it was here that Catesby and four others arrived exhausted in the early evening of 5th November 1605, having ridden from London on relays of horses with news of Guy Fawkes's capture. From there they went to Dunchurch and with sixty others set off for Wales, where they hoped to enlist the help of Welsh Catholics.

Late on 7th November, in pouring rain, they reached Holbeach House near the Staffordshire border. Drying their clothes and ammunition in front of a fire, Catesby and others were severely burned when some gunpowder exploded. Next day the house was surrounded by the High Sheriff of Worcestershire and his men. In the shoot-out that followed Catesby, brave to the end, stood back to back with his wounded friend Thomas Winter until they were both killed by the same musket ball.

OS 152: SP 573682. Ashby St Ledgers is on a by-road 2 miles (3 km) west of A5 at Watford Gap.

Barford Bridge

Since the days of horse-drawn traffic drivers have been alarmed by the ghost of Barford Bridge, which appears as a monk-like figure. Some have stopped, thinking they had run someone down, but have found nothing.

On the by-road from Geddington which joins the A6003 nearby solitary drivers have been joined by a spectral monk. On a foggy night in February

1984 a woman saw in her rear-view mirror what appeared to be a man's face. Thinking it a trick of the light, she looked again, found it still there and drove home much discomforted. A police sergeant had a similar experience and stopped to investigate, thinking someone was in the back seat, but it was empty.

Perhaps these happenings are connected with the former chapel at the vanished hamlet of Barford. This was served by a monk from Pipewell Abbey, which until the Reformation was about 2 miles (3 km) north-west of the bridge. As late as the mid nineteenth century a footpath from Pipewell to the bridge was known as Monk's Walk.

* * * * *

Just past the bridge on the way to Corby there once rose a mound, 12 feet, (3.7 metres) high and 100 feet (30 metres) across, crowned by trees. Though local children played on the hillock by day, all kept away after dark, since at midnight a drummer boy would appear and beat his drum. The mound was excavated and flattened in 1964 and finds suggested that this had been a Roman tumulus; thirteen skeletons are thought to have been secondary burials.

OS 141: SP 861831. The much altered bridge carries A6003, here a dual carriageway, over the river Ise 2 miles (3 km) north of Kettering.

Barnwell

The gaunt shell in front of the great house is all that remains of the castle possibly built about 1266 by Berengarius le Moyne. His name is linked with the grim legend that after a quarrel he walled his brother up here but it is the ghost of a monk with a whip that reputedly haunts the castle.

This is not the only ecclesiastical shade at Barnwell. Once there were two parishes here and some distance away, down a cul-de-sac lane beside a

This gravestone in Barnwell churchyard bears the likeness of a monk. The ghost of a monk has been seen nearby.

stream, is what remains of All Saints church. When the parish was amalgamated with that of St Andrew in 1825 the church was demolished save for the chancel, which was kept because it was the mausoleum of the Earls of Sandwich, a branch of the Montagu family. The graveyard is kept in good order and among the monuments is an ancient slab with what appears to be the likeness of a monk engraved on it. A monk-like figure startled a young man and frightened his dog in this vicinity in the late 1980s.

OS 141: TL 048853 and 048843. Barnwell village is close to A605 where the Oundle bypass leaves the old road 3 miles (5 km) south of the town. The remains of All Saints church are in a lane going south from that of St Andrew and ¹/₂ mile (800 metres) from it.

Blisworth

Blisworth's chief claim to fame is its canal tunnel. When it was completed in 1805 its length of 1³/₄ miles (2.8 km) made it one of the world's wonders.

On 14th September 1861, however, the *Northampton Mercury* recorded an 'awful catastrophe', which had happened on 'Friday evening last'.

Steamboats had just come into use and the *Bee* with two 'engineers' and two 'boatmen' aboard, was passing through the tunnel at 3 mph (5 km/h) when it stopped at a 'stank', where piles had been driven in to make a platform for some workmen who were repairing the tunnel. Here it took on board Edward Webb, a carpenter who lived at Stoke Bruerne at the south end of the tunnel.

Soon afterwards they met two other narrowboats, propelled by 'leggers' (the normal method until 1870 was to have two men lying on a plank and using their feet against the wall to propel the boat through), and behind these was another steamer. At that time there was only one ventilation shaft to take away fumes, so that a dense cloud of smoke was accompanying the *Bee* with a following wind. Webb was suffocated; Broadbent, the boatman who was steering, became insensible and fell into the water, from which his body was retrieved by dredging. The other boatman was still alive when he fell overboard at the mouth of the tunnel and the shock revived him but the two engineers were lying near the furnace, 'awfully burned'.

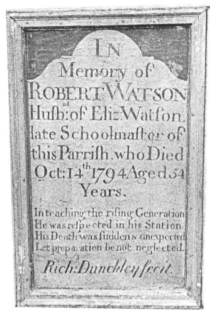

The grave of Robert Watson at Blisworth.

One of the shafts built as a result of the accident is at Buttermilk Hall, a farm above the line of the tunnel, and it has been said that people approaching that spot in the tunnel have experienced a feeling of suffocation and heard the sounds of men choking and drowning as they did so long ago.

* * * * *

In the church of St John the Baptist in Blisworth village is a cautionary epitaph inscribed on a wooden tablet:

IN Memory of ROBERT WATSON Husb:[nd] of
Eliz: Watson, late Schoolmaster of this Parrish,
who Died Oct: 14th 1794 Aged 54 years.
In teaching the rising Generation
He was respected in his Station
His Death was sudden & unexpected
Let preparation be not neglected.
Rich: Dunckley fecit.

OS 152: tunnel SP 739503, church SP 725535. Blisworth has been bypassed by A43 5 miles (8 km) south of Northampton. The tunnel is easily approached from Stoke Bruerne and the Canal Museum, following the towing path opposite the Boat Inn

(where the casualties were taken). The minor road from Stoke Bruerne to Blisworth goes over the hill through which the tunnel was bored and follows its line, passing vents such as the one at Buttermilk Hall. Stoke Bruerne is a short distance from A508 9 miles (15 km) south of Northampton.

Boughton

About half a mile (800 metres) from the village centre and beside the former green stands the ruined church of St John the Baptist, described in Victorian times as a 'picturesque fragment', for the tower and spire fell in 1785. The churchyard is haunted, it is said, in a most unusual manner. According to whether it was met by a man or a woman the ghost appeared as a beautiful girl or a handsome young man and departed after the victim agreed to meet again in a month's time. The promise was sealed with a kiss and the hapless passer-by was doomed.

So when on Christmas Eve in 1875 a farmer named William Parker went that way it was a lovely girl with red hair and blue eyes who invited him to sit beside her and exchange pleasantries, but when she soundlessly departed he knew he would shortly die, as he did a month later on 24th January 1876.

* * * * *

From 1351 to 1916 the famous Boughton Green Fair was held on the green. In June 1826 George Catterall, known as 'Captain Slash', arrived at the fair with a gang of ruffians who brutally attacked victims and robbed them. They were bravely taken on and overpowered by local men and Catterall later appeared in court 'having his head bound up in a silk handkerchief, in consequence of the fracture of his skull. In taking him his left hand was broken and two of his ribs.'

On 21st July he ascended the 'fatal platform', where it is said that he kicked off his boots, to make liars of

Boughton Green Lane, shown on an old postcard.

those who had said he would die in them, before he was 'launched into eternity'.

OS 152: SP 765655. The old church and former green adjoin the minor road from Boughton to Moulton 4 miles (6 km) north of Northampton town centre.

Boughton House

The seat of the Montagu-Douglas-Scott family, whose head is the Duke of Buccleuch, is the largest mansion in the county. Charles Montagu-Douglas-Scott, who was crippled by polio at the age of three, was fascinated by local legends and by 1906 had written 35 versions of them in ballad form. One was the story of the spectral Montagu coach:

> The coachman drives with an urgent rein,
> Yet white is his mien and thin...
> And tomorrow you'll search the gravel for mark
> Of hoof or of wheel in vain.

Another is the story he tells of an ancestor, Ralph, Duke of Montagu. He was the second husband to the wealthy Duchess of Albemarle, who proclaimed on the death of Albemarle that she would marry only royalty. Accordingly Duke Ralph courted and married her disguised as the Emperor of China and, having done so, 'immediately placed her in confinement'. There was a tradition that the unfortunate mad Duchess was at one time shut in the attics of the north-west wing of Boughton House.

OS 141: SP 902815. Boughton House is on A43 3 miles (5 km) north of Kettering.

Braunston

The Admiral Nelson Inn at the canal village of Little Braunston is both picturesque and haunted. Situated in Dark Lane, with a lock hard by, it has a blocked-up doorway through which a 'man in black' has been seen to pass by customers there; whether they were sober or otherwise is not recorded.

Boughton House.

OS 152: SP 549658. Braunston lies beside A45 about 5 miles (8 km) north-west of Daventry. Dark Lane is a cul-de-sac leaving the village main street at its eastern end.

Brigstock

This village gave its name to one of the three bailiwicks of Rockingham Forest where affrays between keepers and poachers have led to many casualties (see Sudborough). In 1252 Matthew, forester of the park at Brigstock, saw men coursing deer at Benefield Lawn. He and his men 'hailed and pursued them. And the aforesaid malefactors standing at their trees turned in defence and shot arrows at the foresters so that they wounded Matthew ... with two Welsh arrows', so that he

The Admiral Nelson at Little Braunston, where a man in black has been seen by customers.

subsequently died. 'Welsh arrows' reminds us that the long bow was a Welsh invention.

* * * * *

The practice of archery may have led to the presence of a strange relic known as the Bocase Stone. It is only 3 feet (1 metre) high but has two inscriptions reading: 'In this plaes grew Bocase Tree' and 'Here stood Bocase Tree'. One of the suggested explanations for this is that 'Bocase' is a corruption of 'bow-cast' and that local men met here to improve their skill in archery.

OS 141: SP 950875. Brigstock is bypassed by the A6116 between Corby and Thrapston. The Bocase Stone is 1¼ miles (2 km) from Brigstock on a broad bridleway on the edge of Harry's Park Wood.

Brington

There are two Bringtons, Great and Little, but to which the universal legend of the three wishes belongs is not clear. A woodcutter was beginning to fell a tree when the elf-like creature who lived inside its trunk offered him three wishes to spare it.

Arriving home tired and hungry at the end of this long day, the wood-cutter thoughtlessly wished for some black puddings for his supper, which immediately came clattering down the chimney. His wife, furious when she learned why this happened, wished

The mysterious Bocase Stone at Brigstock.

Great Brington church and cross.

Memorial near Brixworth to Viscount Chesham who was killed while riding with the Pytchley Hunt.

them on to the end of his nose. There they hung while all attempts to remove them failed. When scissors were used, the woodcutter shrieked in agony, so they were forced to use the last wish to gain relief.

OS 152: SP 667652. This map reference relates to the church of St Mary at Great Brington, near the edge of Althorp Park, a few miles north-west of Northampton. In it is the Spencer Chapel, the mausoleum of the ancestors of the Princess of Wales.

Brixworth

From Northampton the approach to Brixworth is up a steep incline and at the foot of it stands a neglected 21 foot (6.4 metre) high stone cross erected in 1908 to the memory of Charles William Compton Cavendish, Viscount Chesham. He was following the hounds of the Pytchley Hunt in full cry near Daventry when his horse caught its hooves while jumping, fell on him and broke his neck.

* * * * *

All Saints is probably the most impressive early Saxon building in England and contains, amongst much else, a fourteenth-century stone reliquary found in 1809 in a wall in the south (Verdun) chapel. Inside was a small bone thought to be the larynx of St Boniface, the eighth-century English missionary who was known as the Apostle of the Frisians and celebrated for his symbolic act of felling the sacred oak of Geismar, much revered by heathen worshippers. His feast day on 5th June has been celebrated at Brixworth since the mid thirteenth century, when a charter was granted for an annual fair, and a medieval guild of St Boniface was created here.

* * * * *

In late Victorian times the Brixworth Board of Guardians became notorious as the 'Bury-all board'. This was a pun on the name of the chairman, Canon W. Bury, rector of Harlestone, whose policy was to refuse outdoor relief and

The workhouse at Brixworth.

'offer the house' (residence in the workhouse) to needy cases to keep down the rates. Reform followed the election of a new chairman in 1895 so that Brixworth was no longer 'the only union in the county where such a harsh and cruel system prevailed'.

OS 141: SP 750705. Formerly on A508 6 miles (10 km) north of Northampton, Brixworth has now been bypassed. The memorial to Viscount Chesham is 1 mile (1.6 km) north of the Pitsford turn off A508.

Bulwick

On 22nd June 1893 Lady Tryon of Bulwick was entertaining guests in London when some approached her and said how pleased they were that her husband could be present, since they had seen him walking through the assembled company. This was surprising because by then Admiral Tryon was at the bottom of the Mediterranean, where that very day his flagship, HMS *Victoria*, had sunk with the admiral and 357 of his crew, following a collision with HMS *Camperdown*. Why the admiral, considered the finest naval tactician of his day,

13

should have ordered a manoeuvre that inevitably led to this disaster remains a mystery.

The bronze plaque to his memory in Bulwick church is not the only reminder of the Tryons's service to their country, for another memorial records the death of five men of the family in the First World War.

OS 141: SP 963943. Bulwick has been bypassed on the A43 10 miles (15 km) north-east of Corby on the way to Stamford.

Burton Latimer

According to legend the unhappy Lady Isabel Latimer was abducted from the manor house at Burton, to which her family gave its second name, by Lord Seagrave of Barton Seagrave, although she was betrothed to Hugh Neville. When she resolutely refused Seagrave's advances he lodged her in a dungeon until such time as she would yield.

Helped by one of Seagrave's servants, Hugh Neville and Isabel's brother rescued her and set off by night for the castle at Braybrooke, which belonged to the Latimer family. By the time they had reached the ford of the river Ise near Kettering Seagrave and his men, who were in hot pursuit, had overtaken them and in mid-stream a mêlée ensued. In the confusion and terror of the encounter Hugh Neville was killed and Lady Isabel and her brother both drowned. It is said that she haunted Seagrave for the rest of his life and that her ghost was often seen floating like a swan over the water of the ford.

* * * * *

Remote from the town of Burton Latimer but still within the parish is the strange structure known as the Wellington Tower, the Round House or the Panorama. The first Duke of Wellington often stayed with General Arbuthnot and his family at nearby Woodford House and after the final defeat of Napoleon he stopped his carriage at Burton Wold and pointed out to his host the similarity of the terrain to that of Waterloo.

The tower was built as a viewing point with an iron balcony and after various vicissitudes, including a period as a disreputable pub, it is now a private dwelling. In 1913 the resemblance of its surroundings to that of the battlefield was exploited by a film company to re-enact Wellington's triumph. A hundred troopers of the 12th Lancers acted as cavalry and dead horses were brought from knackers' yards and scattered about to lend authenticity to the scene.

The Wellington Tower, also known as the Round House or the Panorama, was built as a viewing point but is now a private dwelling.

Castle Ashby House.

OS 141: SP 884772 (site of ford), 935748 (tower). The tragedy supposedly took place where the A6 trunk road crosses the river Ise near Wicksteed Park. The earthworks of Braybrooke Castle are marked at OS 141: SP 770846. Braybrooke is 3 miles (5 km) west of Desborough on the minor road leading to Market Harborough. The Wellington Tower is 3 miles (5 km) north of Finedon along the A510 and stands alone.

Castle Ashby

The Compton family of this place (Earls of Northampton from 1618) played a considerable part in the Civil War. Spencer, the second Earl, raised his own regiment and while leading a cavalry charge at the battle of Hopton Heath near Stafford in 1643 was unhorsed and surrounded by the enemy, who offered him quarter if he would surrender. This he refused to do, say-

ing he would never surrender to rogues and rebels such as they, and after a fierce struggle was 'knocked on the head'.

His oldest son James, the third Earl, and three of his other sons all played notable parts, a contemporary report saying that 'You will scarcely match these four brothers in his Majesty's dominion'. They showed their mettle in a raid on the Parliamentary stronghold of Northampton when James had his headpiece beaten off, Charles escaped a pistol shot at point-blank range only because of a misfire, William had a horse killed under him and Spencer, sixteen at the time, was surrounded by eight Parliamentary cavalrymen but was rescued by a concerted charge by his brothers so that they all escaped.

Their mansion lies between Newport Pagnell, another Parliamentary stronghold, and Northampton, so that in their absence it suffered an arson attack in which the east wing was severely damaged. To this day burn marks are visible beside the windows on that side of the house. Worse would have occurred but for an old woman who lived in a small room over the north porch of the church, from where she saw the fire and summoned help from the village, so saving the rest of the house.

By 1645 the young Earl had become a notable cavalry commander and led one of the two southern cavalry brigades in the Royalist army. In one foray from Oxford he burned down the manor house at Aynho, also in Northamptonshire, the seat of the Cartwrights, who were Puritans and followers of the Parliamentary cause.

OS 152: SP 863593. Castle Ashby house and village are 2 miles (3 km) north of A428, 7 miles (11 km) from Northampton.

Charwelton

A notorious murder took place here in 1821 and became the subject of a ballad that was current in the county. Among those who sang it was Jack Dickson, a local 'character' who annually entertained the company at Silverstone Harvest Home celebrations with the following:

> Charwelton's in Northamptonshire;
> A gentleman farmer lived there,
> One, Mr Smith; he had a wife
> Who led him a most unhappy life.
> This wicked wretch, we understand,
> Did better love their serving-man,
> And bought a pistol, powder and shot,
> To execute this horrid plot.

And so on, ending with a warning to young men against 'wicked women'.

The real name of the target of the 'horrid plot' was John Clarke, an elderly and wealthy farmer, and it was a shotgun that did the deed. On the afternoon of Saturday 10th February 1821 he was cutting hay from a stack when a blast from a nearby barn wounded him severely in the left arm.

A former army surgeon, Robert Wildgoose of Daventry, amputated his arm but he died at four o'clock the next Tuesday morning.

Before he died Mr Clarke told of his suspicions of Philip Haynes, a former employee who was Mrs Clarke's lover. There had been two previous attempts on his life, once by a rope across the highway and again by a 'blow against his gate' from which he escaped.

Mr Canning, Clarke's executor, had a guard placed round the barn from which the shot had been fired and a search revealed a large hole in the straw, where a gun and other articles were concealed. A further search on Monday discovered Haynes hidden deep in the straw and he was arrested and charged. Before Clarke died he demanded to see Haynes, who asked the farmer how he was 'with great unconcern'. Clarke pointed his remaining arm at Haynes and called out: 'You bloody-minded fellow, how could you do me this unkind office?'

A Daventry constable searched Haynes's lodgings and found a number of letters from Mrs Clarke in which she incited him to murder, as in letter number 47, when she wrote: 'I pray you do all you can to get shut of him ... d—— him, do him if you can.'

The judge's comments on Mary Clarke and her paramour at their trial were severe: 'the prisoners had been convicted of the foul and tremendous crime of murder, ... having been committed by a wife and servant, after a long and libidinous intercourse.' His sentence was that they were to be hanged and afterwards their bodies were to be 'dissected and anatomised'.

The execution took place on Saturday 10th March and Jack Dickson was one of those present.

OS 152: SP 536564. Charwelton is on A361 5 miles (8 km) from Daventry on the way to Banbury. The Clarkes lived at Cherwell Farm on the Hellidon Road but their dwelling has been demolished and replaced by a newer farmhouse.

Clopton

This sequestered village on the eastern fringe of the county was from the fourteenth century until 1764 in the possession of the Dudley family, one of whom returned to disturb the peace in the early years of the twentieth century. The revenant earned the name of 'Skulking Dudley' because his hunchbacked shape was seen on moonlit nights dodging in and out of hedgerows, unable to rest because of a murder he committed in 1349. He 'walked' from Clopton Manor past the former graveyard and the demolished St Peter's church and along the Lilford Road to reach a small coppice, later named after him.

These visits caused such alarm after 1900 that in 1905 the Bishop of Peterborough and 21 other clergy came to exorcise him. After that his wanderings ceased.

Another story about the Dudleys is that of Agnes Hotot, a great heiress who married into the family. Before her marriage her father, Sir John Hotot, was challenged to a duel by one Ringsdale but as Sir John was suffering from the gout Agnes armed herself, took her father's place and defeated Ringsdale. 'When he lay prostrate on the ground she loosened her throat-latch, lifted up the visor of her helmet, and let down her hair about her shoulders, thus discovering her sex.'

OS 142: TL 063803. Clopton is about 4 miles (6 km) along B662, which leaves A605 from Thrapston to Oundle at the Lilford turn.

Corby

Corby was only a village in 1930, but the steel industry caused it to grow into a town of 50,000 people. Nevertheless it has preserved the ancient tradition of the Pole Fair. This is held every twenty years at Whitsuntide (in 1982, 2002 and so on), with an exception in 1985, when the fair was held to mark the four hundredth anniversary of the charter granted by Elizabeth I. The special feature of the fair was that all roads were closed and tollgates were erected; anyone who refused to pay the toll had to 'ride the stang' to the village stocks. This meant that they balanced, legs astride, on a pole carried between two men, a relic of a punishment used by the Danes. Corby is a Scandinavian place-name.

OS 141: SP 880887.

Cosgrove

There is a ghost story connected with the elegant house known as the Priory and a forlorn maiden who once lived there. The tale goes that she fell in love with a young shepherd, an alliance that her parents would not tolerate. So they arranged for him to be arrested on a trumped-up charge of sheep stealing and he was transported, whereupon she drowned herself in the millstream. There on moonlit nights she is sometimes seen.

* * * * *

A more abiding feature is the chalybeate spring known as St Vincent's Well — Fincheswell in the vernacular — the iron content of which is claimed to have great healing properties, especially in the cure of sore eyes. It is recognised as a holy well and safeguarded by Act of Parliament.

Cosgrove Priory.

OS 152: SP 797433. *Cosgrove can be approached from A508 half a mile (800 metres) north of the roundabout at Old Stratford. The Priory is at the end of a cul-de-sac lane after crossing the bridge over the Grand Union Canal and adjacent to the river Tove. The mill has gone. St Vincent's Well is in a field behind the old National School and can be reached from the entrance to Cosgrove Lodge.*

Cotterstock

Late in the seventeenth century this village was the birthplace of Elinor Shaw, the victim of a witch hunt, the record of which gives a chilling insight into her horrific end.

The contemporary account by one Ralph Davis of Northampton says that Elinor was 'left to shift for herself at the age of fourteen years' and by the time she was 21 her character was such that even children would call after her 'There's Nell the strumpet', so that, in common with other so-called witches, she was despised and rejected.

To revenge herself on her detractors, she allegedly sold herself to the Devil, in partnership with her close friend Mary Phillips of Oundle. According to their confessions they were visited on 12th February 1704 about midnight by a 'black tall Man', who told them that if they pawned their souls to him he would get them whatever they desired. He then pricked their finger ends so that they could sign the 'Infernal Covenant' in blood and the same night 'had carnal knowledge of them both'.

Crack's Hill near Crick.

They also confessed that at further visits the Devil presented them with imps and that by the 'Assistance of these Hellish Animals' they killed in the space of nine months fifteen children, eight men and six women. Also they destroyed forty pigs, one hundred sheep, eighteen horses and thirty cows, 'even to the utter Ruin of several Families'.

They were also reputed to be responsible for many 'waggish tricks', including a grotesque episode which occurred after they were imprisoned. A Mr Laxon and his wife looked into the jail and the latter told Elinor Shaw that the Devil had left her in the lurch, whereupon Elinor muttered strangely to herself for about two minutes. Following this Mrs Laxon's clothes were turned over her head, 'exposing her nakedness', despite all her husband's efforts to keep them down, 'at which the said Elinor having Laughed Heartily, and told her she had prov'd her Lyer; her Cloaths began to come to their right order again.'

There was more unseemly laughter on 17th March at the 'Gallows on the North-side of the Town' (of Northampton). When asked to say their prayers the condemned women 'both set up a very loud Laughter, calling for the Devil to come and help them'. The sheriff then ordered them to be executed as quickly as possible 'So that being Hang'd till they were almost dead, the Fire was put to the Straw, Faggots, and other Combustable matter, till they were Burnt to Ashes. Thus lived and thus dyed, two of the most notorious and presumptious Witches, that ever were known in this age.'

OS 141: TL 048905. The village is on a by-road 2 miles (3 km) north of Oundle.

Crick

One former inhabitant of Crick remembers his father speaking of the celebrated 'treacle mines' in the 1920s, since when various additions have been made to this legend. Among them it has been suggested that the M1 motorway was initially built as far as Crick on account of the mines. On occasions implements said to have been used in the extraction of the treacle have been on display and a 'miner' dressed rather like one of the Seven Dwarfs has been glimpsed in the village.

One physical feature relating to the mines is to be found on the Yelvertoft Road, where there is a 'largish conical mound' known as Crack's Hill which has been identified as a spoil heap resulting from the excavations, although more prosaically minded people say that it is the result of the boring of the Crick canal tunnel. Another feature remembered by a former resident was 'a small sewage farm on the Rugby side of the road at the bottom of Buckmills Lane'. Anyone who strayed in this area was 'considered to be in the treacle'.

OS 140: SP 588725. Crick is on A428 a mile (1.6 km) east of junction 18 of the M1 motorway.

Culworth

At about ten o'clock on the morning of Friday 3rd August 1787 a melancholy procession left the County Gaol near the town centre of Northampton on its way to the 'gallows ground' on Northampton Heath. Four of the men in the two carts were leading members of the Culworth Gang. From Culworth, near Banbury, for more than ten years they committed burglaries and high-

way robberies over a wide area of the surrounding counties. One crime concerned a farmer at Sulgrave Grounds: 'one of them, in the Middle of the Night, called Mr Wyatt up, under a pretence of having a Drove of Pigs which he wanted to be taken in; but as soon as Mr Wyatt had got a few yards from the Door, they knocked him down, and one of them stamped upon his Breast, whereby he was most shockingly bruised both on his Head and inwardly'. He was then dragged into the house and shut in the pantry with his wife, while goods and money were taken to the value of more than £40.

The leader of the gang was John Smith, who was of 'great bodily strength and daring energy of character', and his companions on their last journey were William Bowers, William Pettifer and Richard Law. After a probable last drink at the Bantam Cock Inn, then at the outskirts of the town, the tumbrils wended their slow way along the Kettering Road to the Heath, now a public park. There, in the words of a contemporary pamphlet, 'their behaviour was very suitable for persons in their unhappy situation. They all acknowledged the justice of their sentence, and begged the surrounding Multitude to take warning of their untimely End. And about Twelve o'clock they were launched into Eternity.'

The reference to a 'multitude' seems to have been justified, for the *Northampton Mercury* reported that it was 'supposed that more than Five Thousand Persons were assembled' and the population of Northampton in 1801 was only 7020. 'Unseemly behaviour' on such occasions caused the removal of executions to the 'New Drop' at the back of the County Gaol from 1819 onwards.

OS 152: SP 764622. This is the map reference for the Northampton 'gallows ground', which was on the edge of the racecourse, opposite the Kingsley Tavern. Culworth village is about 8 miles (13 km) north-east of Banbury.

The Wheatsheaf at Daventry, prior to its conversion to a nursing home.

Daventry

A most historic haunting occurred at the Wheatsheaf Inn in 1645. The Royalist army arrived in the town on 7th June and Charles I stayed there six nights. According to 'a person of Newarke att that time in his Majesties' Horse', the ghost of the King's former counsellor, Lord Strafford, appeared on two successive nights and warned him not to stay in the vicinity, causing him great unease. 'Prince Rupert, in whom courage was the predominant quality, rated the King out of his approbation the next day and a resolution was taken to meet the enemy.'

After more indecision the King decided to move northward but by then the army of Fairfax was 'upon their rear' and the battle of Naseby followed on 14th June (see **Naseby**). Had Charles gone earlier the history of the Civil War might have been different.

OS 152: SP 576617. The Wheatsheaf Inn continued in Sheaf Street (once the main thoroughfare but now pedestrianised) until 1990, when it was converted into a nursing home. The exterior has changed little so that it is still easily recognisable.

Deanshanger

In 1714 the parish papers recorded a strange accident: 'Chargis of the maid that was killed at the maypole £1.17.6.' Schoolchildren nowadays enmesh their ribbons in patterns on a pole much smaller than the eighteenth-century ones, which were sometimes as high as 40 feet (12 metres). The dancing of the youths and maids was much more rumbustious, so it may be that the pole fell on the unfortunate girl.

OS 152: SP 767395. Deanshanger is beside A422 from Old Stratford to Bucking-

Deanshanger

The village green at Deanshanger.

Deene Park.

ham and the green where this accident probably happened adjoins the road.

Deene

The Brudenells of Deene are an ancient aristocratic family who once held the title of Earls of Cardigan. The seventh and last Earl was the colourful character who led the Charge of the Light Brigade and gave his name to a useful woollen garment.

He is to be seen in effigy in the parish church, along with that of his hardly less remarkable wife, Adeline. She was the daughter of Admiral de Horsey and in her youth mixed with a fast social set, including the notorious courtesan Skittles, who referred to Adeline as 'the head of our profession'. At 33 she became the mistress of the sixty-year-old Earl and on the death of his wife they were united in what would now be called an 'open marriage', for she did not object to the Earl's entertaining other ladies as long as discretion was observed.

As she grew older she became increasingly eccentric. On Cardigan's death in 1868, because she wished to be remembered as a beautiful woman, she had her own death mask made at the same time as her husband's. She kept her coffin in the hall and would lie in it and ask people how she looked. She smoked cigars, when that was a daring thing to do, and rode a bicycle wearing her late husband's uniform with cherry-red cavalry trousers, or went bare-legged with a short kilt. To cover the ravages of time she wore heavy make-up and a blonde wig and, until her death in 1915 at the age of ninety, remained eccentric, witty and popular with local folk.

OS 141: SP 952927. Deene is just west of A43, about 6 miles (10 km) north of Corby.

Eastcote

In 1674 Ann Foster of Eastcote was 'arrained as a witch'. This wretched old woman had allegedly fired the barns and corn belonging to Joseph Weedon and bewitched a flock of sheep and his horses and cattle 'to the utter Ruin and undoing of the said Joseph Weedon'. A contemporary pamphlet goes on to give a revolting description of her imprisonment in Northampton Castle, used as a jail until 1675, and in 'what likeness the Devil appeared to her in Prison' before she was hanged.

When she was chained to a post she swelled up, so she was loosed,' to give her more liberty that the Devil might come to suck her, the which he usually did, coming constantly about the dead time of Night in the likeness of a Rat, which at his coming, made a most lamentable and hideous noise which affrighted the people that did belong to the Gaol', but they 'could see nothing but things like Rats'.

OS 152: SP 680541. Eastcote is a hamlet 1 mile (1.6 km) east of A5, adjoining Pattishall, and 5 miles (8 km) north of Towcester.

Easton Maudit

The Reverend Francis Tolson did not take holy orders until he was 26 because he was first admitted to Lincoln's Inn. He came to Easton Maudit as a curate in 1732 and served as vicar from 1737 until his death in 1745. It was what followed then that has earned him lasting remembrance at Easton Maudit.

Whether there was some irregularity in the arrangements for his burial which disturbed his precise legal mind can only be surmised but, whatever the reason, his ghost was said to have been seen disconsolately wandering by the pond in the vicarage garden. Local legend adds that this clerical shade was finally exorcised by twelve priests throwing thirteen candles into the pond to ensure that he would not walk again until the candles were burnt out.

OS 152: SP 889588. Easton Maudit is on

The remains of a deserted house at Faxton in 1960.

a by-road 2 miles (3 km) east of A509 at Bozeat, which is 7 miles (11 km) south of Wellingborough.

Easton on the Hill

In the far northern extremity of the county, bordering on Lincolnshire, Easton is remote from the City of London but there is a link. In the church of All Saints there is a memorial to a former rector's son, Lancellot Skinner, who went down with the ship *La Lutine* off the Dutch coast in 1799. The ship's bell was salvaged and is now the famous Lutine Bell sounded at Lloyd's of London to announce a maritime disaster.

OS 141: TF 011047. The village stands on the scarp above the river Welland and on A43 road 2 miles (3 km) south of Stamford.

Faxton

There are many deserted village sites in Northamptonshire but one of the most remarkable is that of Faxton, east of Lamport, because it was abandoned within living memory. The 1841 census recorded 108 inhabitants and the Reverend Vere Isham started a school there, but at the 1921 census only 37 people of all ages remained.

The last person born there was George Noble, in 1907, and he remembered a hard existence on his father's small farm. His mother's only respite was when she went on foot to take butter and eggs for sale at Lamport and elsewhere and on her return in winter he would set the dogs barking to guide her home across the mistenshrouded fields. She wanted him to get away from this environment, which he did, and others must have felt the same.

Between the two world wars services were held in the church but it then fell into disuse, was vandalised and in 1959 demolished. All habitation has now gone and only a memorial stone marking the site of the church remains. Some notable memorials were removed to the Victoria and Albert Museum, including one with a remarkable history.

This was to Sir Augustine Nicholls, lord of the manor from 1608 until his death eight years later. It was not the first time the monument had been moved. Nicholls was a judge on circuit at Kendal when he was supposedly poisoned by four women on the eve of the trial of a relative of one of

24

them, in the belief that in this way they would prevent the death sentence. His handsome memorial was installed in Kendal church but by Victorian times had been relegated to a lumber room. From there it was rescued by the former curate of Faxton, the Reverend J. Wilkinson, and the Reverend R. Isham of Lamport and remained at Faxton until 1959.

OS 141: SP 784754. 1¹/₂ miles (2.4 km) north of Old, on the minor road going towards Loddington, a field track on the left leads to the site of Faxton at a distance of ³/₄ mile (1.2 km).

Fotheringhay

Few small villages have so many tragic royal associations. The founder of the House of York, Edmund Langley, was given the manor by his father Edward III. He had the idea of a college there and his son Edward, the second Duke, established it in 1411 but

he was killed at Agincourt in 1415 and was buried in the church.

In the Wars of the Roses Richard, Duke of York, claimed the throne after the battle of Northampton in 1460 but in the same year he was captured at Wakefield and, after being crowned in mockery with a 'wreath of grass', was beheaded along with his son Edmund. Later another son, the Earl of March, afterwards Edward IV, brought back to Fotheringhay the bodies of his father and brother. Solemn ceremonies were enacted and in more recent times people have claimed that they heard the ghostly strains of melancholy medieval music. Cecily Neville, the mother of these sons, is also buried there. Another son, the future Richard III, spent the first six years of his life at Fotheringhay.

When Elizabeth I visited the church she found the graves of her Plantagenet ancestors in disarray and in 1573 ordered the building of the two identical and imposing monuments.

All that remains of Fotheringhay Castle, bearing a plaque to Mary, Queen of Scots, who was executed there.

25

Mary, Queen of Scots, during her many years in prison.

Here also took place the last act in the tragic history of Mary, Queen of Scots. It was preceded by a catalogue of mishaps in Scotland: her ill-fated marriage to Lord Darnley in 1565; the murder of her Italian secretary Rizzio in 1566; Darnley's death after being blown up by gunpowder at Kirk o' Field in 1567; the rash and hasty marriage to the thuggish Bothwell only three months later, which swung the Scots lords against her and led to her imprisonment at Loch Leven, from which she escaped to cross the border and throw herself on the mercy of Elizabeth I in 1568.

In a letter to Elizabeth she prayed not 'to be made the sport of Fate' but this is what she became. For nearly twenty years she was moved from one place of detention to another, often in living conditions which undermined her health, until she finally reached Fotheringhay. All this time her presence caused concern to Elizabeth and her advisers because many Catholics saw Mary as the rightful Queen of Eng-

land and a possible restorer of their faith. Babington's plot to assassinate Elizabeth and free Mary, to which she appeared to agree, was the signal for her trial in 1586 and Elizabeth's reluctant assent to her execution.

Tall, beautiful and accomplished in language, literature and music, nothing became Mary better than her end. The execution was timed for eight o'clock on the morning of the 8th February 1587, a bitterly cold day. Clad in black, Mary calmly climbed the platform set up in the Great Hall of Fotheringhay Castle, heard the death warrant read, then took off her black gown revealing a scarlet robe beneath. She kneeled to lay her head on the block and commended her soul to God.

What followed was less seemly. It took three blows to sever her head and when the executioner grasped her auburn hair it proved to be a wig and her head fell to the floor, showing her grey hair; she was only 44. Her little dog then emerged from beneath her skirts and refused to leave her side. Subsequently the organs were taken from the corpse and buried secretly in the castle so that they could not be claimed as relics and the Queen's body was sealed in a lead coffin where it remained for six months prior to burial in Peterborough Cathedral.

In 1612 her son, James I, installed her remains in a sumptuous white marble tomb in the south aisle of King Henry VII's Chapel in Westminster Abbey. Although much of Mary's life was one long disaster she established through her son a royal line of succession lasting until the present day. As she herself said: 'In my end is my Beginning.'

The massive motte of the castle still looms over the river Nene but all that remains of the stonework is a small section with a plaque attached. Other reminders of the unhappy queen are the huge thistles said to have been planted to remind her of Scotland and Garden Farm, where Bull, her executioner, is believed to have stayed in the room over the archway.

OS 142: TL 062930. Fotheringhay is 3½

miles (6 km) north of Oundle on the minor road to Wansford.

Gayton

St Mary's church has several recumbent effigies, including one in oak of a knight thought to be Sir Philip de Gayton, who died in 1316. There are also two of females, the larger supposedly Lady Scholastica de Gayton (died 1354), and a tiny representation on the corbels above her of a child, Mabilla de Murdak.

Lady Scholastica was the daughter of Sir Philip, the last of the de Gaytons. In 1316 it was certified that Thomas Murdak and his wife Scholastica were lords of Gayton. One story says that she murdered her first husband, Sir Geoffrey de Meaux. Another version claims that Scholastica was blameless and that it was her sister Julianna who poisoned her own husband and was burned as a witch as a result.

OS 152: SP 707548. Gayton is on a minor road 2 miles (3 km) north-west of A43 at Blisworth.

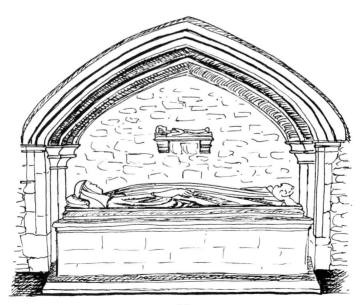

The Eleanor cross at Geddington.

Geddington

In 1290 Queen Eleanor, wife of Edward I, died near Lincoln and her embalmed body was brought to London for burial. The king ordered a cross to be built in her memory at each overnight stopping place on the journey — the Eleanor crosses. Of the nine built only three original crosses survive: at Geddington and near Hardingstone in Northamptonshire, and at Waltham Cross in Hertfordshire, the cross at Charing Cross in London being a nineteenth-century replacement. The cross at Geddington is the most complete and forms a fine centrepiece to the village.

OS 141: SP 896829. Geddington is adjacent to A43 4 miles (6 km) north-east of Kettering. The cross is in the centre of the village near the Star Inn.

Grafton Regis

In medieval times the Woodvilles held the manor here and Elizabeth Woodville married Edward IV at Grafton in 1464. This led to a succession of calamities. Her father, Earl Rivers, two of her brothers and her two sons all perished either in the Wars of the Roses or in the events that led to her brother-in-law, the Duke of Gloucester, succeeding to the crown as Richard III. Her sons were the young 'princes in the tower' Edward V and the Duke of York, who disappeared in the Tower of London while in the custody of their uncle, the Duke of Gloucester, who thereupon seized the throne.

OS 152: SP 759469. Grafton Regis is 9 miles (15 km) south of Northampton on A508. In the church of St Mary is the tomb-chest with an incised slab of Sir John Woodville (1415).

Great Harrowden

In the days when Roman Catholics were persecuted there were a number of 'popish recusants' among the gentry of the county and the Vaux family of Great Harrowden were prominent among them. Lady Elizabeth Vaux showed unflinching courage and loyalty to her faith when she sheltered Father Gerrard, her chaplain, at Harrowden Hall.

Nicholas Owens, a lay brother and ingenious carpenter (who later died under torture in the Tower of London), had constructed a 'priest hole' which defied the most rigorous search. This began on 12th November 1605, and for several days Gerrard was cramped in a 'hole within a hole', unable to stand upright but never found. The hiding place still exists, although now boarded up, in the former hall, now the clubhouse of Wellingborough Golf Club.

OS 141: SP 882708. The clubhouse is just off A509 on a minor road to Finedon, 2 miles (3 km) west of Wellingborough.

Grendon

One of the most curious episodes in the history of National Hunt racing is associated with Grendon. In 1901 a horse named Grundon, trained by Mr Bletsoe at Grendon Hall, won the Grand National in remarkable circumstances. The course was under a thick covering of snow and the other horses suffered from balled-up hooves, so that they could not gallop. Grundon, however, with a pound of butter lubricating each hoof, led uniquely from start to finish.

OS 152: SP 880607. Grendon is 3 miles (5 km) west of A509 from Bozeat. The hall, now the County Youth Centre, lies beside the minor road leading to Wollaston.

Guilsborough

Eight years after James I, 'a great detector of demoniacs and the arch enemy of the devil', had passed the Act of 1604 which prescribed the death penalty for those convicted of witchcraft, five so-called witches were hanged on Abington gallows on 22nd July 1612. Their story was told in *The Witches of Northamptonshire*, printed in London by Thomas Parfoot for Arthur Johnson in the same year.

On Helen Jenkinson was found the 'insensible marke which commonly all witches have in some privy place or other on their bodies'. Mary Barber of Stanwick was said to be 'monstrous and hideous both in her life and actions'. Arthur Bill of Raunds was accused of bewitching to death Mary Aspine and to have had 'familiars' named Grissill, Ball and Jack but died proclaiming his innocence.

Agnes Browne and Joane Vaughan, mother and daughter, made themselves objectionable to 'respectable' folk in Guilsborough and paid dearly for it. The accusation said that when Joane Vaughan made offensive remarks in the hearing of 'Mistress Belcher' the latter was so incensed that

she struck her. Joane then swore revenge and later her 'victim' was seized with 'such a gnawing and griping in her body' that her sufferings were pitiable.

When her brother went to confront the women he was prevented from entering their house by some unseen presence and on his return suffered similar symptoms to those of his sister. But the strangest allegation was that Agnes Browne, in company with two others, Kathleen Gardiner and Joane Lucas, and 'all birds of a wing and abyding in the towne of Guilsborough did ride one night to a place (not above a mile off) called Ravenstrop [Ravensthorpe] all upon a sowe's back, to see a Mother Rhoades, an old witch who dwelt there'.

This uncommon feat is depicted in a woodcut on the front of the contemporary pamphlet, an enlargement of

'A Brief History of Witchcraft', published 1866, had an illustration of the Guilsborough witches on its title page.

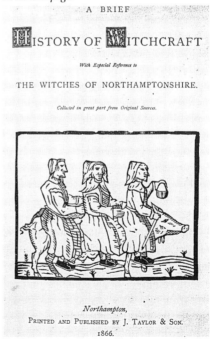

A BRIEF

HISTORY OF **W**ITCHCRAFT

With Especial Reference to

THE WITCHES OF NORTHAMPTONSHIRE.

Collected in great part from Original Sources.

Northampton,
PRINTED AND PUBLISHED BY J. TAYLOR & SON.
1866.

which hangs in the village hall. As late as the 1880s there was supposed to be a 'witch family' in the village.

OS 141: SP 676727. Guilsborough is a mile (1.6 km) east of A50 10 miles (15 km) north of Northampton.

Hannington

The story of the restless ghost of Hannington is well documented. In 1675 Justinian Isham wrote from Christ Church, Oxford, to his father at Lamport that 'The report of the Hannington ghost was spread all over Oxford.' A contemporary pamphlet was headed:

'The Rest-less Ghost or Wonderful News from Northamptonshire and Southwark. Being a most true and Perfect account of a Persons Appearance that was Murdered about two Hundred and Fifty years ago.'

It goes on to say that William Clarke, a maltster of Hennington(sic), who lived at the Old Pell farmhouse, suffered inexplicable happenings. Finally there appeared the spectre of William Pell, who said he had been a farmer and was 'Murthered' nearby 'Two hundred sixty and seven years, nine weeks and two days ago'. The ghost had hitherto been constrained by a friar from walking but was now determined that Clarke should go to Southwark, where Pell had buried money in a house he owned.

Further visits by the ghost caused Clarke to go to London and after meeting the ghost on Southwark Bridge he was directed to a house where Pell's descendants still lived and where the ghost reappeared and set Clarke to work digging in the cellar. There at a depth of 8 feet (2.4 metres) he unearthed a metal box containing gold and silver coins and a parchment verifying the story.

The pamphlet said that the ghost appeared at Southwark not only to Clarke but to 'several others, on Sunday last the tenth of this instant January' and that the account 'will be Attested and Justified by Will Stubbins, John Charlton, and John Stevens, to be spoken with any day, at the Castle Inn without Smithfield-Barrs, and many others'.

OS 141: SP 813710. Hannington is a small village a mile to the west of A43 midway between Northampton and Kettering.

Hardingstone

Shortly before 2 am on 6th November 1930, two young men of Hardingstone, William Bailey and Alfred Brown, returning home from a Bonfire Night party, saw a great blaze at the side of the lane which led to the village from the London Road from Northampton. A man, respectably dressed and carrying a briefcase, appeared from the hedge and, when they asked him what the fire was, he said it was a bonfire, before heading towards the London Road. When the young men

The grave of an unknown man murdered at Hardingstone.

reached the fire they saw it was a blazing motor car and quickly fetched the village policeman.

In the passenger seat was the charred body of a man whose identity was never discovered. In the ditch adjacent to the car was found a wooden mallet, and other suspicious circumstances set the police looking for the owner of the car, registered number MU 1468.

They soon caught up with Alfred Arthur Rouse, a commercial traveller, who had got a lift to London. While at Hammersmith police station he boasted about his 'harem': there were at least three other women in his life apart from his wife. His trial for murder began 23rd January 1931, in the courthouse in George Row, Northampton, and attracted nationwide publicity. It became plain that Rouse had attempted the faking of his death as a means of escape from his many entanglements. At 8 am on 10th March he was hanged in Bedford jail and buried in an unmarked grave in the prison grounds.

Ten days later, at 5 am, the maids at the Vicarage in Hardingstone were woken by the sound of digging in the churchyard and, peeping through the curtains, they saw the sexton preparing a grave before a strange funeral took place by lamplight. Only 'official observers' were present as the vicar laid to rest the sad remains of Rouse's victim, which had remained in a bath of formalin in Northampton General Hospital for four months. Secrecy was maintained to avoid public interest, of which there was plenty, for a constant stream of visitors passed by the grave at the weekend.

In June 1931 an oak cross costing £14 was placed over the grave and a casket buried at its foot containing a record of the trial. The inscription on the cross reads: 'In memory of an unknown man, died 6th November 1930.'

* * * * *

Another macabre, although less gruesome, episode occurred at Hardingstone

in 1923, when the village schoolmaster, Mr Blick, died. His corpse was laid out in the schoolhouse and his pupils filed in two by two to view his body and 'pay their last respects'.

OS 152: SP 763578. Hardingstone is now within the bounds of Northampton. The Hardingstone Lane, leading from the London Road to the village, begins at a huge roundabout giving access to several arterial roads and what was in 1930 a lonely road is now lined with houses.

Hargrave

Three Shire House is where the county boundary of Northamptonshire meets the borders of Bedfordshire and Cambridgeshire (formerly Huntingdonshire). It was the scene of two unusual interments. In 1837 the wife of an eccentric farmer died and since there was some difficulty concerning her burial in Hargrave churchyard, her husband having quarrelled with the parish priest, he had her body bricked up in the house. In 1845, following the death of a daughter, he did the same and it was not until he himself died 24 years later that his son was able to transfer the remains to a burial ground.

OS 141: TL 047705. The house is a mile (1.6 km) from the village along A45 going towards St Neots and stands beside a water tower.

Harrington

Lady Jane Stanhope, whose family held the manor of Harrington in the first half of the seventeenth century, was a keen gardener. She also possessed a violent temper, so that when an old gardener (of whom she was fond) roused her wrath she lashed out and killed him with a blow from a spade.

Instant and lasting remorse followed, so that on occasions the wraith of a 'White Lady' is seen floating at twilight over the terraces where once the

The Tollemache Arms inn at Harrington.

gardens were. This is a sight to be avoided, for the legend says that those who see it have not long to live.

* * * * *

The Stanhopes were followed by the Tollemaches, the family of the Earls of Dysart. A member of this family was the Reverend Hugh Tollemache, rector for 58 years until he died aged 87 in 1890. He thought it ungodly for his parishioners to attend the inn on Sundays so he bought it, installed his coachman as landlord and closed it from Saturday night until Monday morning. Corpses were laid out in what is now the restaurant of the Tollemache Arms before removal for burial at the church.

OS 141: SP 773803. Harrington is 3 miles (5 km) east of A508 at Kelmarsh. As you enter the village a wall and horse-chestnut trees on the left screen the Falls Field, the name given to the site of the remains of the former mansion. A bridleway leads to it.

Heathencote

On 16th June 1776 a certain Captain Fleming was made to 'stand and deliver' by a highwayman near Pottersbury, south of Towcester on the 'Liverpool Road' (now A5). He then returned to Stony Stratford, got a fresh horse and accompanied by a post-boy galloped north in pursuit of the robber. On the way they were joined by the Reverend John Risley of Tingewick, who was armed with a pistol.

Near Heathencote, a mile (1.6 km) south of Towcester, they overtook the highwayman and called on him to surrender. Instead of doing so he drew a pistol and fired at them but missed. The post-boy then called on the parson

and several watches were on him, but no means of identification, and he was buried in Towcester churchyard the following night.

The third Duke of Grafton, whose seat was at Wakefield Lodge near Potterspury, was so impressed by the courage and marksmanship of the Reverend John Risley that he gave him the living of Ashton, which he held until 1799. He then retired in favour of his son and became personal chaplain to the Duke for the rest of his life.

OS 152: SP 710472. Heathencote is still a tiny hamlet today, just south of Towcester.

Kilsby

When Robert Stephenson engineered the London & Birmingham Railway — the first main line — in the 1830s the biggest difficulty was the creation of the Kilsby tunnel. Quicksands and springs caused repeated flooding and thirteen pumping engines worked day and night for over nineteen months

to shoot back and his aim was better, for the villain tumbled from his horse, stone dead.

His body was carried down the hill to Towcester and lodged in the Roundhouse lock-up. Three loaded pistols

The top of a ventilation shaft in Kilsby tunnel.

Kilsby

The church at King's Sutton.

before it was overcome.

A shanty town grew up above the tunnel accommodating 1250 navvies in foul turf huts. These men worked hard, drank hard and sometimes rioted; then soldiers from Weedon barracks were fetched to subdue them. Two main ventilation shafts 60 feet (18 metres) in diameter were constructed from the tunnel and in a drunken frolic three navvies fell over 100 feet (30 metres) to their deaths. Their ghosts are thought still to haunt the shaft.

OS 140: SP 569708. Kilsby is on A5 south-east of Rugby. One ventilation shaft with a crenellated top stands on the north side of A5 ½ mile (800 metres) east of the village.

King's Sutton

Penda, the last pagan king of Mercia, is believed to have had a royal household at King's Sutton. His reputed grandson St Rumbold (or Rumwold)

was born of Christian parents in the seventh century. He was the most extraordinary of early saints for, although he lived only three days, in that short time he is said to have eloquently preached Christianity. A spring feeding a well in a field near the railway station is named after him and still gives good drinking water.

Rumbold's name also still lives on at Brackley and Buckingham, where in turn his remains were subsequently buried and where also springs are dedicated to him, while at Buckingham a street bears his name.

OS 151: SP 496361 (St Rumbold's Well). King's Sutton is on the western extremity of the county near Banbury, separated from Oxfordshire only by the river Cherwell, and 2 miles (3 km) north of B4100 near Aynho.

Lamport

The squire of Lamport for most of the Victorian era was the eccentric Sir Charles Isham, the tenth baronet, who in 1847 imported model gnomes from Nuremberg and displayed them on a giant rockery in the garden of Lamport Hall. An attempt is being made to renew the rockery but only one of the original gnomes remains — on display indoors.

OS 141: SP 760745. Lamport Hall is on A508 9 miles (15 km) north of Northampton.

34

The stocks at Little Houghton.

Little Houghton

Little Houghton is one of several Northamptonshire villages to have kept its stocks. Others are Aynho, Eydon and King's Sutton, but in the case of Little Houghton it is known who was the last occupant. In the late nineteenth century William Baucutt was lodged in them for beating his wife.

OS 152: SP 803597. The village has been bypassed, so now lies off A428 3 miles (5 km) east of Northampton. The stocks are in the main street near the post office.

Lois Weedon

The Reverend William Losse became vicar here in 1618 and continued in office until 2nd July 1643, when twelve Parliamentary troopers came from Northampton to arrest him, on account of his Royalist beliefs. They arrived in the middle of a service and the vicar would not go quietly. One of the soldiers told him that he might ride behind him or otherwise he would drag him along with a halter at his horse's tail but Losse defied them and climbed up into the belfry and so on to the roof by means of a ladder which he pulled up after him to deny his pursuers similar access.

There 'he resolutely and successfully defended his post; they discharged their pistols at him eight or nine times, but fortunately missed their aim; they wounded him however in several places with their swords, and one of

The church at Lois Weedon.

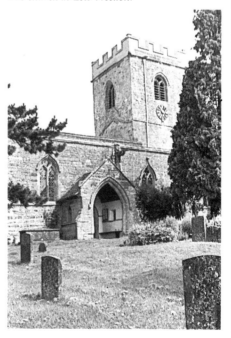

35

his wounds having opened a vein, his blood flowed so fast upon his assailants underneath, that they concluded they had dispatched him and left him to his fate.'

Whether or not he died is unknown and no parish registers exist of that time but in 1899 a brass tablet was erected to record the fate of one of the seven thousand clergymen who suffered under the Commonwealth regime.

OS 152: SP 602470. The village is shown on maps as Weedon Lois but the inhabitants prefer to reverse the name. It stands in a network of lanes 8 miles (13 km) west of Towcester via Abthorpe and Wappenham.

Mears Ashby

Belief in witchcraft continued here as late as 1785, when the *Northampton Mercury* reported on 1st August: 'Thursday last, a poor woman, named Sarah Bradshaw, of Mears Ashby, who was accused by some of her neighbours of being a Witch, in order to prove her innocence, submitted to the ignominy of being dipped, when she immediately sank to the bottom of the pond; which was deemed incontestable proof that she was no witch ... in these more enlightened times, it must show the greatest weakness and cruelty, to accuse any person of a crime, which in its very nature, is absurd and contrary to reason and common sense.' Sarah Bradshaw was fortunate to survive her ordeal, but there is a local belief that her ghost walks in the neighbourhood.

OS 152: SP 838667. Mears Ashby is 2 miles (3 km) north of A4500, 6 miles (10 km) east of Northampton.

Naseby

The climactic battle of the Civil War was fought here on 14th June 1645. The Royal army, under the command of Charles I's nephew Prince Rupert of

the Rhine, the 'King's General', made its stand here against the New Model Army, a well disciplined Parliamentary force superior in numbers. Prince Rupert chose an advantageous position on Dust Hill, 2 miles (3 km) north of Naseby along the Sibbertoft Road, where there is a farm still known as Prince Rupert's Farm. The wind was at his back so that it would blow the smoke of gunfire into the enemy battle lines. These also were athwart the same road, near the spot where in 1936 a monument was erected which erroneously claims that Cromwell's decisive cavalry charge started from that point when it began well to the east of it.

Rupert led the Royalist cavalry on the right wing in a fierce charge against the opposing Parliamentary left and drove most of them off the field but wasted time attacking the baggage train at the rear. Meanwhile Cromwell and his Ironsides on the Roundhead right had seen off the opposing Cavaliers and wheeled in disciplined formation to attack the exposed flank

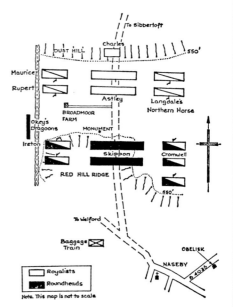

The battle of Naseby, 1645.

The incorrect inscription on one of the monuments commemorating the battle of Naseby.

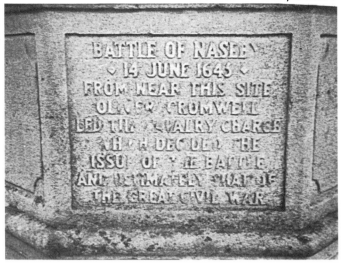

The incorrect inscription on one of the monuments commemorating the battle of Naseby.

of the Royalist centre so that the infantry there were either killed — Rupert's élite troops known as the Bluecoats fought to the last man — wounded or captured. Many of the prisoners were marched to Northampton and imprisoned in the churches there. The King's cause never recovered from this crushing defeat. To round off the blood-letting, two hundred wretched female camp-followers of the Royalist army were slaughtered, Cromwell allowing this to happen on 'grounds of moral principle'.

A solid reminder of the events leading up to the battle, the so-called Cromwell Table, which was in the former inn (now Shuckburgh House) opposite the church, has been moved to the church of All Saints. The officers of the King's rearguard were gathered round it when the army had retreated northwards before the battle and were surprised by the Parliamentary advance guard led by Ireton. More nebulous is the legend that for years after 1645 there were times when people witnessed the struggle re-enacted in the sky, accompanied by all the harrowing sounds of mortal combat.

Following the Naseby Enclosure

Award in 1823 and the resultant ploughing, a poem was written in Latin which mentions — in somewhat flowery English translation — discoveries made by a farmer on the battlefield. He was 'amazed' by 'the broken swords, javelins, eaten away by the decay of age and helmets riddled by bullet marks' and terrified to hear the 'snap of bones as he turns his harrow'. As late as the 1890s bullets and other detritus of battle were still to be found.

OS 141: SP 694800. Naseby village is 2 miles (3 km) east of A50 10 miles (15 km) north of Northampton. There is a museum of the battle at Purlieu Farm (telephone: 0604 74021).

Nether Heyford

On the south wall of the church of St Peter and St Paul is an opulent monument to a judge, Sir Richard Morgan (according to Pevsner), who died in 1556. Others claim that it commemorates Sir Francis Morgan, another judge, who died in 1559. One of these sentenced to death Lady Jane Grey in 1554 and since Sir Francis was not el-

37

The tomb in Nether Heyford church commemorating the judge, probably Sir Richard Morgan, who sentenced Lady Jane Grey to death and later died in a distraction of remorse.

evated to the bench until 1558 it seems most likely that it was Sir Richard who was so distracted by the death of the unfortunate young girl that 'he is said to have gone mad, crying out in his fits, "Take away the Lady Jane from me"; and in this distraction ended his life.'

OS 152: SP 660587. The village is a mile (1.6 km) south of A45 just to the west of the junction 16 of the M1 motorway.

Newton-in-the-Willows

In 1607 about a thousand men gathered here under the leadership of a man known as 'Captain Pouch' — so called because he carried a great leather pouch in which, he told his followers, 'there was sufficient matter to defend them against all comers'. They threw down the hedges surrounding enclosures made by the Tresham family.

This brought swift and brutal retribution from the local gentry and their mounted followers. When 'Captain Pouch' was captured there was found in the pouch only a piece of green cheese. His name was John Reynolds and he and some of his followers were hanged, drawn and quartered and the grisly remains were displayed at Northampton, Oundle and Thrapston.

OS 141: SP 885833. On a by-road to the west of Geddington, the deserted village site has on it only the former chapel of St Faith's (now a field study centre) and the massive dovecote belonging to the Tresham mansion that once stood here.

Northampton

This ancient market and county town has a long and stirring history, little of which, apart from its medieval churches and street names, is evidenced today. Northampton has its own particular saint and martyr. During the reign of Edward the Confessor in the eleventh century the priest in charge of the church which preceded the present Norman church of St Peter was named Brunning, or Brunigus. One of his servants had a dream instructing him to tell his master to dig in the floor of the church, where he would find the tomb of 'the chosen friend of God'. Also present when Brunning began to dig was a crippled beggar woman from Abington named Alfgiva.

When the tomb was revealed the church was filled with a great light and a snow-white dove appeared and plunged into the font before sprinkling Alfgiva and the tomb with holy water. The cripple was made whole and when the coffin was opened the bones were found to be those of Ragener. The nephew of King Edmund, who, according to tradition, was killed by Ingvar the Dane in AD 870 for refusing to renounce his faith, Ragener too suffered martyrdom.

St Ragener's shrine became the resort of pilgrims and a late fifteenth-century will indicates that it was still preserved at that time. A revival of interest resulted in a sung Eucharist in his honour in November 1984 and one of the bells in the new church of St Benedict on Hunsbury Hill was named after the Saxon saint and martyr.

* * * * *

The only structural remains of the great medieval castle which stood on the site of the railway station consist of a postern gate re-erected in a wall nearby. The castle was the place of confrontation between Henry II and Thomas à Becket in 1164, after which the Archbishop fled secretly to take refuge in France. Local tradition says that on his way he paused beside a spring in the Bedford Road. In 1843 this was enclosed in a Victorian Gothic structure and is known as Becket's Well.

* * * * *

Becket's Well.

In the mid thirteenth century Northampton was one of the largest towns in England, the area enclosed within the town walls being third in size after London and Norwich. In common with those cities and with Lincoln, there were pogroms against the Jewish population of Northampton. Following an accusa-

This postern gate is all that remains of the fabric of Northampton Castle. It was removed and reset in the wall near the railway station.

39

The monument to Robert Browne at St Giles, Northampton.

House of York (white rose). Battle was joined in the water meadows beside the river Nene near to Delapre Abbey. Since Henry was not a fighting man, his army was marshalled by his queen, Margaret, and the Duke of Buckingham in strongly entrenched positions with their backs to the river. Initially this gave them an advantage but when the Earl of Ruthin, the queen's cousin, who was commanding the right flank, suddenly switched sides the Lancastrian forces suffered a disastrous defeat. 'Many were slain, and many fled, and were drowned in the river.' It was said that the Nene ran red with blood. The Queen escaped but Buckingham was slain and the King taken captive to London.

* * * * *

tion concerning the supposed murder of a Christian boy on Good Friday 1277, a number of Jews were drawn 'at the horse-tail' to a spot outside the town walls and there hanged. The belief that Jews practised child murder was widespread and long-lasting.

In the next year a general attack on the Northampton Jews for allegedly clipping and forging coin was made and this led to the forfeiture of property and the execution of more of them. Envy, greed and the fact that they were traditional scapegoats played a part. Shylock's character in Shakespeare's play *The Merchant of Venice* embodies what was then the common concept of the race.

In 1282 another gruesome sight appeared in the town when it was 'favoured' with one of the quartered portions of the body of David of Wales, the last sovereign prince of one of the most ancient ruling families in Europe.

* * * * *

During the Wars of the Roses there was a major battle just outside the town. In 1460 the army of Henry VI, representing the House of Lancaster, whose badge was a red rose, clashed with that of the Earl of March, later Edward IV, who led the faction of the

One of the most turbulent priests in the rise of Nonconformity was the Reverend Robert Browne, founder of the Brownists or Independents (later Congregationalists). He boasted of having seen the inside of 32 prisons and died in the jail in Northampton Castle in 1633, having been brought there in his bed at the age of eighty, following an assault on a constable. He is buried in St Giles' churchyard and his monument stands outside the south front of the church.

* * * * *

Above the portico of All Saints' church in the town centre is a statue of Charles II, wearing the unlikely combination of a Roman toga and a full-bottomed wig. It is a reminder of the Great Fire of Northampton in 1675, when more than six hundred houses burned, along with the medieval All Saints, where 'All-hallows Bells jangled their last doleful Knell'. To help the rebuilding of the town Charles granted 1000 tons of timber from Whittlebury Forest and remitted the payment of Chimney Money for seven years. In gratitude the statue was installed and on 29th May (Oak Apple Day) the verger climbs up and adorns the statue with a garland of

40

On 29th May (Oak Apple Day) the verger of All Saints' church, Northampton, places a garland of oak leaves on the statue of Charles II.

An extract from the Northampton Mercury in 1720 giving a gruesome account of the causes of mortality in London over a period of ten days.

[3]

Northampton Mercury.

London: The Weekly Bill of Mortality, From Tuesday, April 19, to Tuesday, April 29, 1720.

Abortive	1	Head-ach	1	Small Pox	—
Aged	46	Headmouldshot	1	Spleen	2
Ague	2	Hooping Cough	1	Stilborn	2
Apoplexy	1	Horseshoe-head	2	Stone	2
Asthma	2	Jaundice	1	Stoppage in the Stomach	2
Cancer	1	Loosenefs	1	Suddenly	5
Childbed	5	Lunatick	1	Swine Pox	1
Confumption	65	Meafles	2	Teeth	1
Convulfion	143	Mbrtification	4	Tifick	8
Dropfie	14	Pleurify	1	Twifting of the Guts	1
Fever	94	Rafh	1	Worms	2
French Pox	3	Rickets	4		
Griping of the Guts	9	Rifing of the Lights	2		

Chriften'd 331; Buried 515. Decreafed in the Burials this Week 20.

CASUALTIES.

Drowned in the Wet Dock, at St. Mary at Rotherbith, 2. Found dead; one in a Coffin, at St. Bennet, Paul's Wharf; and one in a Well at St. Olave in Southwark. Executeder. Kill'd 3 one accidentally, by the Wheel of a Waggon, at St. Saviour in Southwark, and one by the Wheel of a Cart, and one by the Kick of a Horfe, at St. Giles's in the Fields. Overlaid 1. Suffocated in a Wafh-Tun, at St. Saviour in Southwark, 1.

oak leaves. This commemorates the occasion when Charles, in flight after defeat at the battle of Worcester in 1650, hid in an oak tree to escape the Parliamentary soldiers. Within living memory boys at Northampton who did not wear a sprig of oak on this day were subject to rough justice, such as having stinging nettles lashed across them.

Beneath the portico between 1841 and 1864 there was sometimes seated a small man with a massive forehead and a distracted manner. This was the peasant poet John Clare, who in that period was lodged in the lunatic asylum (now St Andrew's Hospital) and during lucid intervals was allowed into the town. During this time he wrote much lovely poetry, including the captivating verse of 'Little Trotty Wagtail'. Some of his other poetry describes the cruelties of country life in his day. In 'Badger' there is a horrific description of badger-baiting when this was a 'sport' and a public spectacle.

* * * * *

In 1892 a gruesome murder case caused a great sensation. The victim was a young woman called Annie Pritchard, whose headless and armless body was found by James Chapman while walking his dog on 7th August 1892. The corpse was wrapped in a sack and hidden in a ditch on the Northampton to Rugby road, just beyond Althorp railway station, on the way to East Haddon. Her married lover, Andrew George MacRae, was a very inept murderer, for on the sack was stencilled 'E. M. MacRae, Northampton, L. and N. W. Railway', which led the police to a bacon-curing establishment in Dychurch Lane owned by MacRae's brother and to a stall in the Market Square where MacRae was arrested while selling bacon.

According to elderly folk in East Haddon who had talked to those living at the time of the murder, the pathetic remains were taken to the premises which were then the Red Lion Inn (since resited) and this local lore sheds a bizarre light on the forensic efforts of the day, for it is said that an attempt was made to establish the date of death by counting the number of maggots to the inch on the corpse. Annie Pritchard had a child by MacRae; its body was never found but in a copper in the cellar of the bacon factory remains of human tissue and hair were discovered and in the firegrate underneath there were fragments of bone.

MacRae was found guilty on Christmas Eve 1892 and hanged in Northampton jail, which was then on the Mounts. But that was not the end of the affair. On occasions people on the road where Annie's remains were found have been followed by footsteps, to their great discomfort, and it has been suggested that they belong to the ghost of the unhappy woman following in her killer's footsteps on his way back to Northampton.

There was some dispute over where Annie's remains should lie but an obscure corner of the cemetery at East Haddon was finally allotted and a headstone was provided by 'Friends and Sympathisers' with an inscription ending 'I was a stranger and you took me in'.

Some of this information was contained in an article written by the late L. W. Dickens — then the doyen of Northampton journalists — in the *Chronicle and Echo* for Wednesday 24th August 1977. He also gave details of a haunted inn, the Black Lion in St Giles' Street, which seemed particularly subject to strange happenings. These include: inexplicable shadows behind glass partitions; an apparition of a man with a big black dog in a bedroom; an occasion when a landlady met a female spectre clad in an old-fashioned riding habit on the stairs; the utter reluctance of any dog to enter the cellar and the time when an 18 gallon (82 litre) beer barrel was moved off its stand and no sound heard.

OS 152: SP 7560.

Orlingbury

Jack of Badsaddle was the nickname of John de Withmayle, both Badsaddle and Withmayle being places in Orlingbury parish. He was a prodigious hunter in Rockingham Forest and, according to legend, he saved the life of the reigning monarch, who was unhorsed in the path of a huge wild boar. Also it is claimed that on this or another occasion he killed the last wild boar in England. Local belief is that his memorial is in Orlingbury church, where there is an alabaster effigy of an armoured knight dated to *c*.1375. If this is correct it would mean that the rescued monarch was Edward III, who reigned from 1327 to 1377.

OS 141: SP 860723. Orlingbury is approached from A509 3 miles (5 km) north of Wellingborough. Badsaddle and Withmale (spelling varies) are 2 miles (3 km) further west.

Oundle

One of the most prominent buildings in this handsome old market town is the Talbot Hotel. In it is a staircase said to have come from Fotheringhay Castle (although close examination shows no sign of a move). Even so, people have claimed to have seen a female figure in a black dress and to have heard a woman

The yard of the Talbot Hotel, Oundle. The large mullioned window lights the haunted staircase.

crying at night, a reminder of the fate of Mary, Queen of Scots.

At the back of the Talbot runs a lane which continues through the inn yard to join West Street. This is Drumming-well Lane, named after a well that before it was filled in during the late eighteenth century used to emit at intervals a sound similar to a rhythmic drumming. Local belief was that the noise was heard before the deaths of Oliver Cromwell and Charles II and prior to the Great Fire of London, and so it was thought to presage calamities.

OS 141: TL 035882. The town is now bypassed by A605: to reach it, leave this road 6 miles (10 km) north of Thrapston.

Passenham

The author's early youth was spent near this shrunken village and he heard in the 1920s talk of the ghost of 'Bobby Bannister'. The spectre was even used as a threat by foolish mothers to try to control refractory children. Sir Robert Banastre was a well authenticated historical character, who grew rich as Clerk Controller in the royal household in the early seventeenth century. He left a handsome memorial in the church of St Guthlac, where he created the 'faire chauncel' (1626-8) in which his bust, possibly by Nicholas Stone, gazes at the splendour and an inscription says that 'he served three princes in places eminent'. Despite this benevolence, historical records show that he was of a hard and grasping nature

and he certainly left an evil folk memory in the neighbourhood. In 1856 a penny pamphlet appeared saying: 'after his disease(sic) so often he repeated his visits in that neighbourhood, that six men, eminent for piety, were required to lay his spirit, once and for ever afterwards, in the bottom of the mill dam.'

The author has never heard of anyone who actually saw Banastre's ghost but the proximity of the village to the river Ouse with its winter mists make it a place ripe for such beliefs.

A more plebeian shade figures in the tale of Nancy Webb, a local girl who drowned herself in the mill race and whose screams as she was crushed by the mill wheel have been subsequently heard — or so it is said.

* * * * *

Passenham was briefly in the fore-front of national history when it became a forward base during the English re-conquest of the Danelaw, the part of the country ruled by the Danes, the boundary of which was the Watling Street. The Anglo-Saxon Chronicle recorded that in AD 921 'King Edward went with the levies of Wessex to Passenham, and encamped there whilst the fortress at Towcester was being reinforced by a stone wall.' Earlier in the year the English garrison at Towcester had beaten off attacks by the Danish armies from Leicester and Northampton and while at Passenham Edward received the surrender of the Danes of the latter town.

The inscription on the tomb to Sir Robert Banastre in St Guthlac's church, Passenham.

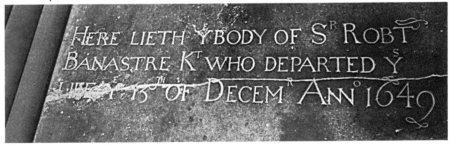

On at least four occasions during the nineteenth and twentieth centuries skeletons have been unearthed in the village outside the bounds of the churchyard. According to a reputable history of Passenham, 'expert examination' showed that some of them were of young men who had met violent ends, so it may be that they were casualties from among the 'Wessex levies'.

OS 152: SP 780394. The Passenham Lane leads off the A422 Buckingham road a mile (1.6 km) south of the junction with A5 at Old Stratford.

Pattishall

In reporting the Timber Stealing Riots of 1727 a forest official wrote: 'There is one Mr Welch, a clergyman, that sent his team and servants on a Sabbath Day to fetch a tree that was cut down by other persons that could not carry it away ye day before; we can prove this, but can't tell where ye timber now is, but is supposed to be concealed by ye parson, and a stack of hay set upon it.'

When the 'other persons' who had cut the tree down went to remonstrate with the parson he threatened 'to shoot any of 'em that should come upon his ground' so that 'they durst not venture'. A later report stated: 'I can get no other information (his own Parish being all afraid of him).'

The Reverend John Welch, who died as vicar of Pattishall in 1752, was succeeded by his son, grandson and great-grandson, the last dying as incumbent in 1872.

OS 152: SP 670543. Pattishall is on A5 5 miles (8 km) north of Towcester.

Paulerspury

Paulerspury adjoins the Watling Street, or Holyhead Road as it was known in the heyday of stage-coach travel. 23rd December 1840 was a very cold day and Richard Andrews, a seventeen-year-old youth from Shrews-

The grave of Richard Andrews, Paulerspury.

bury, got down from a slow-moving coach to run and warm himself. In so doing he slipped, fell under the wheels and was killed instantly. His tombstone is to be seen on the north side of St James's churchyard.

OS 152: SP 715455. 2 miles (3 km) south-east of Towcester along A5 (Watling Street). The church is a mile (1.6 km) from the main road at the end of the long village thoroughfare.

Pitsford

Now known chiefly for the huge reservoir nearby, the village once saw the continuance of an old tradition. Within living memory, on May Day there were chosen not only a May Queen and King but a mysterious figure called 'Jack in the Green'. A boy wore a cane construction about 4 feet (1.2 metres) high with leather straps inside to fit over his shoulders. This was made by a blind man in the village and covered by branches of laurel, barberry and other evergreens; it was possibly a reminder of the Elizabethan 'man in the oak'. Some have erroneously connected this figure with the name of the many inns called the Green Man and with the figure that appears in carvings in churches, depicted as a face surrounded by foliage, one example in Northamptonshire being in All Saints church at Flore, only 12 miles (19 km) from Pitsford.

OS 152: SP 755682. Pitsford is a short distance east of A508 5 miles (8 km) north of Northampton.

Puxley

The name of this hamlet, formerly in Whittlebury Forest, has a sinister ring, for its meaning is 'Goblin's leah' — the clearing where one might meet a goblin, or even worse. The word 'Puck' appears in various spellings in Irish, Welsh and medieval English as a name for the Devil, so that Puxley must have been a truly haunted place. Even today, with Milton Keynes visible on the far horizon, it still has a feeling of remoteness and in the eighteenth century there were happenings in an alehouse there which led to the expression 'Puxley law'.

A man named John Windmill refused to finish his drink and his companions

Puxley.

agreed 'that a man was to be hanged that refused to drink off his cupp'. Percival, the miller at Passenham, was judge and others were sheriff, jury and so on. They got a cord and hanged Windmill but he was saved by the landlady, Jane Thompson, who said 'they would spoil her cord and cut the cord and let him down else he had died'.

This resulted in High Court trial for 'an unlawful and Ryotous assembly ... in contempt of Justice'. The fate of the miscreants is unknown but 'Puxley law' was the term used locally afterwards if a man refused to drink up his glass.

OS 152: SP 758714. Puxley is a mile (1.6 km) north of A422 at Deanshanger along a narrow minor road. Bryant's map of 1827 shows the Fox and Hounds in the vicinity of Hanger Lodge but it has long since disappeared.

Raunds

Known once as 'the home of the British Army boot', the town has a long history of shoemaking. At the time of the Enclosure Act, 1794-6, riots were led by the shoemakers. The Reverend James Tyley, who described the aftermath of the Naseby enclosure, made harsh remarks about the riotous men of Raunds: 'To such, brawls and din and mad riot are dear, and all hatred of

Kings, and contempt of sacred law.' They 'burst from their noisome hovels, abandoning their unfinished soles' and destroyed the hedges and fences and filled in the ditches, crying 'long live the cottagers' rights and the cause of the down-trodden people!' Their efforts were in vain, for the enclosures were soon replaced and the shoemakers 'received their well-merited punishment in prison'.

OS 141: TL 000731. Raunds lies off A605 3 miles (5 km) north of Higham Ferrers.

Ringstead

In 1850 Lydia Attley was made pregnant by a married butcher, Weekley Ball, and on the night of 22nd June she disappeared after visiting him in his orchard. Ball was naturally suspected of her murder and a nine-verse ballad, 'The Cruel Butcher of Ringstead', was written. It began:

Come listen to me and a story I'll tell concerning
of Lydia Attley
Who in Ringstead should be
Chorus: O cruel butcher, he hung should be,
For the killing of Lydia Attley.

Ball was arrested but no trace of Lydia's body was found and so he was released for lack of evidence. His business was boycotted and he left the village.

In February 1864 a female skeleton was unearthed by a labourer digging a ditch in Keystone Lane and Ball was rearrested. Then other bodies were found nearby and it was thought they were the remains of gypsies who used the area, so Ball again went free. The ghost of Lydia was said to haunt the area for twenty years. It would walk from the orchard to the church and then to the spot where the female skeleton was found.

OS 141: SP 985752. Ringstead is now bypassed by A605 5 miles (8 km) north of Higham Ferrers.

Rockingham

A folk tale tells of three brothers who lived in Rockingham village. They were visited in turn by a gnome-like hairy creature called the Redman who was begging for food. The stupid older brothers drove him away but the youngest and cleverest trapped and fed him, keeping him imprisoned until he revealed the location of some crocks of gold in an underground chamber. Thus enriched, the young man was able to buy a fine house at Barn Hill, Stamford, and to marry the prettiest girl in Rutland.

* * * * *

During the Civil War the owner of Rockingham Castle, Sir Lewis Watson, suffered from both sides. First the castle was bombarded by Fairfax's artillery and then stormed by the Parliamentary forces. Charles I was so displeased by its loss that he had Sir Lewis imprisoned in Belvoir Castle. Two portraits, painted before and after these unhappy years, show how his misfortunes aged him.

47

The gatehouse of Rockingham Castle.

The descendants of Sir Lewis still live at the castle and in Victorian times Charles Dickens wrote *Bleak House* while staying there with his friends Mr and Mrs Richard Watson. The castle appears in *Bleak House* as Chesney Wold, the home of Lady Dedlock, and the novelist thought he saw a ghost pass between the Tudor yew hedges and disappear at the iron gate leading to the Wild Garden. It was up this path that the Roundheads advanced when they took the castle.

OS 141: SP 866914. Rockingham is on A6003 a mile (1.6 km) north of Corby.

Rockingham Forest

A strange poaching incident was recorded in the proceedings of the Forest Court held in 1272. A number of men went on a foray, including Ralph of Heyes, the bailiff of the Earl of Warwick at Hanslope, and Henry, the son of the parson at Blisworth. They were in such force that the keepers fled and could not resist them. After killing three deer, they cut off the head of a buck, transfixed it on a stake in the middle of a clearing and placed an object in its jaws so that 'it made the mouth gape towards the sun, in great

contempt of the lord King and his foresters'.

It may not have been merely 'contempt'. Thirteen men were named in the indictment — the number of a witches' coven — and it could be that they were perpetuating an old ritual using the antlered head of a buck. A relic of this ritual, the Abbots Bromley Horn Dance, lingers to this day in Staffordshire.

The fragmented remains of Rockingham Forest still stretch from just north of Kettering to Duddington, a distance of 20 miles (32 km).

Rothwell

Rowell, as it is locally known, has the longest church in the county (173 feet or 53 metres) but is best known for another reason. The nickname of the Rothwell Town soccer team is 'Bones', because beneath Holy Trinity church is a bone crypt or charnel house stacked with skulls and thigh bones. It lies beneath two bays of the south aisle and measures 30 feet (9.1 metres) long by 15 feet (4.6 metres) across and $8^1/2$ feet (2.6 metres) high.

This medieval relic was forgotten

until 1700, when, according to local tradition, a gravedigger fell into it. In 1910 the skulls and thigh bones were arranged neatly and compressed into a smaller space, these particular relics having been kept in the belief that they were necessary at the Resurrection. To view this macabre spectacle one must attend the church between 2 and 4 pm any Sunday from Easter to September.

OS 141: SP 816812. Rothwell is on A6 4 miles (6 km) north-east of Kettering.

Rushton

Much of the history of this place is bound up with the Tresham family, of whom Sir Thomas (1534-1607) left his mark in buildings such as the Triangular Lodge, shaped by his fervour as a Roman Catholic convert and full of religious symbolism. Everything about it is in threes, representing the Holy Trinity and exhibiting the Tresham trefoil badge. His faith cost him fifteen years in prison as a 'popish recusant' and led to his son Francis's involvement in the Gunpowder Plot in 1605.

It was thought that Francis Tresham sent the cryptic warning letter to his brother-in-law Lord Monteagle which led to the discovery of the plot: 'for they shall receive a terrible blow and yet shall not see what hurts them'. This belief has been queried but there is no doubt that he perished miserably in the Tower of London. He did not suffer execution like some of his fellow conspirators but died from a lingering and painful disease on 23rd December 1605. The Lieutenant of the Tower was ordered to have his head cut from his body 'and so used by some skilful surgeon that it may be preserved till further directions be given'. Later it was

The bone crypt or charnel house at Rothwell.

The Triangular Lodge at Rushton.

displayed on one of the gates of Northampton.

In 1619 the estate was sold to Sir William Cockayne. The head of this family later became Viscount Cullen and two legends concern the family and Rushton.

In the first a fiddler was employed to try to trace the course of a tunnel supposedly running from the Triangular Lodge to Rushton Hall, playing as he went so that his course could be followed above ground. The music stopped and those who tried to traverse the tunnel found it blocked by a fall and the fiddler was seen no more.

Numerous fanciful variations have been created on this theme but Charles Montagu-Douglas-Scott (see Boughton House) gives a very prosaic explanation: in the Lodge were three apertures, two filled by cupboards and the third blocked by stonework, and the latter gave rise to the notion of a tunnel.

The other story concerning the Cockaynes has more foundation in fact. Charles Montagu-Douglas-Scott said that in the mid seventeenth century Bryan Cockayne, heir to Charles, the first Viscount, was betrothed to Elizabeth, the daughter of Sir Francis Trentham. He then went abroad to complete his education, where he 'seems to have forgotten the fact of his betrothal', as Scott delicately puts it.

He returned and the marriage festivities were in full swing at Rushton Hall when a 'southern lady' appeared and laid a curse on her faithless lover. Lord Cullen, as he became, went into exile, ruined and broken-hearted, and his wife died in want at Kettering almshouses in 1713.

OS 141: SP 833830. The Triangular Lodge, maintained by English Heritage, is off A6 2 miles (3 km) east of Desborough on the minor road to Rushton. Rushton Hall is now a school.

Salcey Forest

Until 1991 the county boundary between Northamptonshire and Buckinghamshire ran through the smallest of the three ancient royal forests of the former county. This led to one of the most notorious episodes in the history of prizefighting. On 23rd July 1830 Alexander McKay, known as the 'Highland Hercules', and Simon Byrne were matched to fight with bare fists at Hanslope, Buckinghamshire, which parish borders on Northamptonshire. There McKay was lodged at an inn, the Watts Arms.

Salcey Forest.

The local constables tried to stop the fight so the pugilists and their followers crossed over the county boundary and battled for 47 rounds at Salcey Green at the edge of the forest. By then McKay had received such a beating that he was carried back to the Watts Arms on a handcart and died there the following day. Byrne was tried for murder at Buckingham assizes but rich followers of the prize ring hired such an array of lawyers to defend him that he was acquitted amid great acclaim by his supporters.

OS 152: SP 800520. The easiest access to Salcey is via B526 7 miles (11 km) south of Northampton.

Scaldwell

In Scaldwell a Grey Lady is sometimes seen, so called because she is dressed in grey clothes of Victorian style, with a veil of the same colour. This is reputedly the ghost of Madeleine Smith, a young Edinburgh woman who was the central figure in an unresolved murder mystery.

51

Scaldwell

In July 1857 she was arraigned in a nine-day trial charged with the murder by poison of her former lover, Emile L'Angelier. She was the daughter of a wealthy Edinburgh architect and he the son of a Jersey nurseryman who was working as a packing clerk. She had written him a number of letters, the unrestrained passion of which caused a sensation, but later ceased to love him. She was alleged to have poisoned him with doses of arsenic, strong enough to kill forty men, in coffee and cocoa. Evidence was given that she had bought arsenic on the pretext that she needed it to kill rats at the family country house but following an eloquent plea by her defence counsel the jury brought in a 'not proven' verdict after only 25 minutes.

To get her away from the scandal surrounding her name at Edinburgh she was sent to stay in Scaldwell, where a relative was rector.

OS 141: SP 770725. Scaldwell is on a minor road 1 mile (1.6 km) east of A508 and 2 miles (3 km) north-east of Brixworth.

Silverstone

The Reverend C. D. Linnell, a native of 'Silson', as it was locally known, grew up there in Victorian times and later wrote a book entitled *Old Oak* full of the stories handed down to him. One concerned an ancestor named Saywell who farmed at the former site of Luffield Abbey, all traces of which were removed when the wartime airfield was built which later formed the nucleus of the motor-racing track. In 1740 Saywell was plagued by deer from Whittlebury Forest, among them being a buck with a face like that of a man, which repeatedly disappeared at the same spot. When the farmer dug there he unearthed a treasure, which Linnell suggested had been buried by the monks in times of trouble. The story does not relate what happened to this wealth subsequently.

OS 152: SP 673442. The village lies on the western side of A43 road 4 miles (6 km) south of Towcester. Luffield Abbey was situated on the land where the motor-racing track now is.

Percy Pilcher with his sister Ella and one of his gliders.

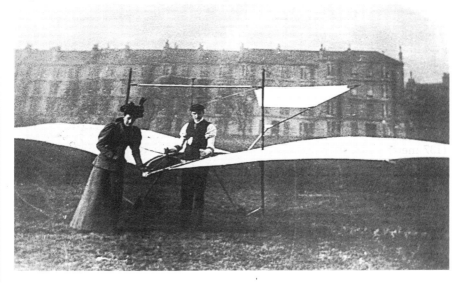

52

The 'dun cow bone' at Stanion church — actually a whalebone.

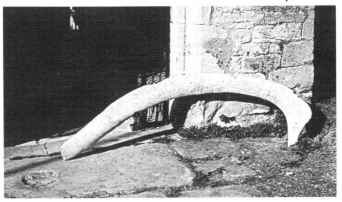

Stanford-on-Avon

The river Avon at Stanford divides Leicestershire from Northamptonshire. Stanford Hall is in Leicestershire but the village is in Northamptonshire, as also is the monument to Percy Pilcher, a former naval officer and pioneer of flying.

In 1899 he was present at a house party at Stanford Hall, with the intention of demonstrating the possibilities of his glider, the *Hawk*, a bird-like structure which had previously travelled airborne for 400 yards (365 metres) and risen to a height of 50 feet (15 metres). He was also experimenting with powered flight, building a triplane to be driven by an internal combustion engine.

On Saturday 30th September, despite rain and strong gusty winds, Pilcher went ahead with his attempt. At 3.40 pm a team of horses (or servants, according to another account) pulled on the apparatus to get the glider airborne but it had gone only about 150 yards (137 metres) and risen 30 feet (9 metres) when a sharp gust of wind snapped part of the bamboo framework so that the glider turned over and hit the ground with Pilcher trapped underneath. He died of his injuries the following Monday.

OS 140: SP 593793. Stanford-on-Avon is a few miles north-east of Rugby. The

Pilcher monument is about 100 yards (90 metres) to the left of a bridleway leading from the direction of Park Farm north of Stanford village to cross the river. It bears two inscriptions: on one side, 'Percy Pilcher, Pioneer of Aviation fell here on Sept. 30, 1899'; and on the other 'Icaro Alteri' ('another Icarus').

Stanion

In the church of St Peter there is what appears to be a whalebone 5 feet (1.5 metres) long. This is supposedly the rib of a gigantic cow that once supplied milk to the whole village. A local witch ended this benefit by milking the cow through a sieve so that, exhausted by its continuous output, it died and was buried in a field known as Cowthick.

OS 141: SP 915868. Stanion is close to Corby, south of the town and adjacent to A43.

Stowe Nine Churches

Various reasons have been advanced for this curious name, among them being the lord of the manor here once had the right of presentation of clergy to nine parishes. More colourful is the legend that seven times the men of Stowe tried to build a church at the foot of the hill on which the village stands and every time their work was vandalised during the night. On the eighth occasion an intrepid peasant kept watch by night but in the darkness could see only that the destruction was wrought by a 'crettur no bigger nor a hog', but with supernatural strength. This convinced the builders that they must shift to the hilltop, from where the Saxon tower of St Michael's church looks over a wide prospect of the upper valley of the river Nene.

OS 152: SP 638577. Church Stowe (the parish also comprises Upper Stowe, where there is a Victorian church) lies a short distance west of A5 (Watling Street) and a mile (1.6 km) south of Weedon Bec.

Sudborough

The village is in Rockingham Forest and so has a long history of poaching. The best-known episode is concerned with 'Poacher Mays' and is told in a ballad still sung in folk clubs to this day.

On Monday 9th January 1837 25 Sudborough men went poaching at Deenethorpe, where fourteen keepers, acting on a tip-off, confronted them. The affray that followed left one poacher dead and three captive.

At the inquest on Wednesday 11th January it was found that William Mays died from 'over-exertion', but when the trial of his confederates took

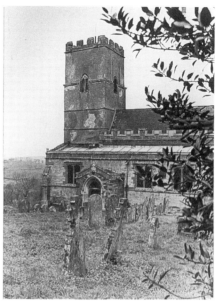

The church of St Michael at Stowe Nine Churches.

place on 27th February doubts were cast on the coroner's verdict. The keepers gave evidence that the Sudborough men were armed with 'bludgeons' and guns but when asked if they themselves carried spears one keeper denied doing so himself but admitted he had heard that others were so armed.

The Wesleyan chapel at Syresham.

54

There was no doubt in the mind of the ballad writer:

> Then to injure the poachers
> The keepers they did start
> And in that strife took poor Mays' life —
> They stabbed him to the heart.

* * * * *

Until his death in 1990 Sudborough was the home of Denys Watkins-Pitchford (better known as BB), who grew up at Lamport, where his father was rector, and who in later life became celebrated as a writer, artist and compiler of books dealing with country matters. According to his obituary notice he was the victim of a curse. As a young unmarried cleric, his father visited the Holy Land, where unhappily he refused alms to a beggar. The latter swore that neither the clergyman's first son nor the first son of his second male offspring would reach manhood. Engel, Denys's older brother, died as a schoolboy and Denys's own son Robin did so at the age of eight.

BB's home at Sudborough was in a circular former tollhouse, dated 1660, which is noticeable on entering the village from the direction of Thrapston.

OS 141: SP 967821. Sudborough has been bypassed by A6116 from Thrapston to Corby 4 miles (6 km) north of Thrapston.

Syresham

John Kurde, a shoemaker of Syresham, was Northamptonshire's sole Protestant martyr. He was living in Northampton when the law for burning heretics was revived in 1555 and when he denied the doctrine of transubstantiation, the Catholic belief that the bread and wine of the Eucharist become the actual body and blood of Christ, he was imprisoned in Northampton Castle. His trial took place in All Saints church, Northampton, in August 1557 before William Binsley, Archdeacon of Northampton, and he was condemned to death. In September Sir Thomas

Tresham, the sheriff of the county, made the arrangements for his execution. The vicar of St Giles, John Rote, tried hard to persuade Kurde to recant but despite the offer of a pardon he refused and was led out of the north gate of the town and burnt to death in the stone pits on the way to Kingsthorpe.

In Syresham he is commemorated by a plaque in the Wesleyan chapel.

OS 152: SP 630415. Syresham adjoins the north side of A43 5 miles (8 km) north-east of Brackley.

Sywell

The 1884 Derby horse-race was won by a horse called Running Rum. A protest was lodged alleging that he was a four-year-old, that is a year too old to be eligible to compete. A lawsuit followed but Running Rum could not be found. The story goes that he was brought to Sywell by night, slaughtered and buried in the grounds of Sywell House. In court the judge was brazenly told: 'You will never see the horse again, but you may have a quarter of him if you like.'

Some say that the rattling of phantom buckets and the clip-clop of spectral hooves have been heard as the ghost of the unfortunate horse is led into the yard of Sywell House.

OS 152: SP 821673. Sywell is a mile (1.6 km) east of A43 and 5 miles (8 km) north-east of Northampton.

The tomb of Archdeacon Sponne in Towcester church bearing two stone effigies of Sponne, the one underneath representing a gruesome cadaver.

Towcester

Archdeacon Sponne was rector of St Laurence's church from 1422 to 1448. He created a benefaction to start a grammar school (his name continues as the title of the comprehensive school which has succeeded it) and funded the building of the Chantry House near the town hall. But his most dramatic relic is his monument in the church. It consists of an effigy above and a cadaver below: a telling reminder of mortality.

* * * * *

A legend of a spectral hunter (see Introduction) is associated with Towcester and nearby Whittlebury Forest. A girl from the town jilted a young huntsman, who in despair killed himself. She married another but before long she also died and her ghost was later seen forever fleeing from the 'Wild Hunter' and his phantom pack through the woodland that stretches

away past Silverstone towards Brackley.

OS 152: SP 695488. Towcester, the site of the Roman station of Lactodorum on the Watling Street, is where A43 crosses A5 7 miles (11 km) south-west of Northampton.

Twywell

The Reverend H. Waller of this parish knew two of the most eminent Victorian figures. When General Gordon, later to be killed at Khartoum, visited the Holy Land in 1880, he sent his clerical friend three stones from the site of Calvary, where Christ was crucified, and these are to be found in the splay of the window to the right of the altar in the church of St Nicholas.

The parson also enjoyed the friendship of Dr David Livingstone and displayed in a glass case in the church are pieces of bark within which was carried the embalmed body of the mis-

Wappenham

The church of St Mary has an unusual feature, a one-handed clock thought to be of the time of Elizabeth I. In the 1640s, at the time of the English Civil War, the parish had probably the most notorious parson in the history of the county.

The lord of the manor in 1642 was Robert Wallop, a keen Parliamentarian, and he ejected the rector and installed one Theophilus Hart, who was not even in holy orders. In 1650 Wallop sold his property in Wappenham and most of it ended in the hands of Hart, mainly by sharp practice.

When Charles II was restored Hart held his post by bribing the bishop's secretary with £5 and a brace of bucks and hired a curate to read services and dig his garden. But his most scandalous conduct was his liaison with the wife of the local butcher. A village history recounts that the butcher, George Tarry, chased him on several

The three stones from the site of Calvary, surmounted by a cross, at Twywell.

sionary by his faithful followers, Susi and Chuma, on their journey to the coast.

OS 141: SP 952782. Twywell is ½ mile (800 metres) north of the A604 Kettering to Thrapston road 3 miles (5 km) west of the latter.

Memorabilia of David Livingstone at Twywell church, including the pieces of bark in which Livingstone's followers carried his body on their journey to the coast.

occasions over hedges and ditches without success, but he finally caught the pair in bed and ended Hart's infamous career with a meat axe. By then the ungodly parson had reached the age of 65.

OS 152: SP 625458. This village is 6 miles (9 km) west of Towcester on a very minor road.

Weedon Bec

Here are holy connections, both pagan and Christian. 'Weedon' means 'the hill with a temple or sacred place' and 'Bec' derives from when the manor belonged to the monks of Bec Hellouin in Normandy.

In the Dark Ages, about AD 700, a nunnery was founded here by St Werburga, daughter of Wulfhere, suc-

This window in Weedon Bec church depicts St Werburga and the geese.

cessor to Penda as king of Mercia. Tradition says that Werburga was pursued by numerous suitors on account of her beauty but chose instead the life of a nun.

Her name is associated with a strange legend. In the words of Michael Drayton (1563-1631) in his verse 'Polyolbion', described by him as a 'chorographical' description of Great Britain:

Saint Werburga, princely born, a most religious maid,
From these peculiar fields, by prayer, the wild geese drave.

She freed the village of a plague of geese which were eating all the crops and even brought back to life a goose that had been killed and cooked by a peasant when the other geese would not leave without it. As late as the eighteenth century, according to Morton's *Natural History of Northamptonshire*, there was a 'vulgar superstition' that no wild geese were ever seen to settle and graze on 'Weedon field'.

OS 152: SP 634593. Weedon Bec is at the intersection of A45 and A5.

Weekley

This village is only a mile (1.6 km) from Boughton House and so within the bounds of the estate of the Montagu (now Montagu-Douglas-Scott) family, some of whose opulent tombs are in the parish church. Ralph, first Duke of Montagu, who had been ambassador in Paris under Charles II, employed a Dutch gardener, Van der Meulen, to lay out formal gardens and these were embellished by a series of pools and fountains and a spectacular cascade of five stages, all of which culminated in a large pond called the 'Grand Etang' in front of the mansion. The pond is now only a rectangular depression in the ground.

If the traces of this watery complex are followed to its source near the fringe of Weekley, there is, hidden in a clump of bushes, a weather-beaten

The statue known as 'Stone Moses' at Weekley. It is said to come to life at midnight.

Wellingborough

During the English Civil War, while Northampton was a Parliamentary stronghold, Wellingborough favoured the Royalist cause and this led to a minor but bloody encounter. When the Roundhead Captain John Sawyer led his troops into Wellingborough in 1642 he was greeted by a charge of goose shot (heavy duty shot) in the head and neck, so that he fell on his horse's neck, and was attacked, according to a Royalist pamphlet, by a 'Countryman', who with a club beat him off his horse into the dirt'.

The account goes on: 'the Women to avenge their Husbands Quarrel fasten on him', but he was rescued by two 'gentlemen' or 'otherwise had immediately died the death of Sisera, by the hands of Women'. Sawyer lived for only two hours and before long his brother, Captain Francis Sawyer, arrived with reinforcements, hell-bent on revenge. Seeing Mr Flint, a curate of Harrowden, near the fatal spot, he 'barbarously struck him with his Pole Ax' and 'cleft his head down to the eyes'.

statue with its base in a pond. Here was the spring feeding the system. Locally known as 'Stone Moses', the statue is said to come to life and go down to the river Ise for a drink when Weekley church clock strikes midnight.

OS 141: SP 890806. Weekley is on A43 2 miles (3 km) north of Kettering. As you enter the village from the direction of Kettering a cul-de-sac lane leads off immediately to the right for about ¾ mile (1.2 km). Near the end of it a short distance from its right-hand side is the copse wherein 'Stone Moses' is concealed.

Weldon

On the green here is a roundhouse or lock-up, with a conical roof topped by a stone orb, and a single massive and heavily studded oak door. Such small jails were once more common (see Heathencote). A local undated memory is that of an old man who remembered that as a boy he and others would throw stones through the grille of the tiny window to torment the prisoner inside.

OS 141: SP 928894. Weldon is a mile (1.6 km) east of A43, leaving Corby on the way to Stamford.

The roundhouse or lock-up at Weldon.

Whittlebury church.

OS 152: SP 892680. Wellingborough is 12 miles (19 km) from Northampton along the new A45 dual carriageway and a little nearer by the old road (now A4500).

Welton

In 1658 incredible things happened to the younger of the two daughters of Widow Stiff of Welton. She began by vomiting water and, having brought up 3 gallons (14 litres), regurgitated a vast quantity of stone and coals, some lumps weighing as much as a quarter of a pound (113 grams), so that they could hardly be passed from her mouth.

This went on for a fortnight, during which time, according to the report, flax would not burn on the fire, the bedclothes sprang off, objects were spun about, milk was spilled and pellets of bread were thrown around. Then a suspected witch was sent to jail and the widow and her daughter were little troubled afterwards.

Another unfortunate child is buried in the churchyard. There is the grave of a six-year-old boy who was found starved to death in 1806.

OS 152: SP 581660. The village adjoins

B4036 from Daventry 3 miles (5 km) north of the town.

Whilton

Like Wappenham, Whilton has a curious Elizabethan church clock, in this case with only four minutes marked on each five-minute interval. Also, it once had a very eccentric rector.

In his will in 1783 the Reverend Langton Freeman decreed that after his death he should be left in his bed until his body had 'grown offensive'. Then his corpse should be wrapped in a 'strong double winding sheet' and laid in his bed in the summerhouse in the garden, as near as possible to the fashion of 'Our Saviour's' burial.

The building was to be locked up, planted round with evergreen plants, fenced off with iron or oak pales and painted dark blue. All this was done in October 1783, and the bizarre relic was still present in the 1870s but there is no trace of it today.

OS 152: SP 636647. The village is just north of the Roman road which ran from Duston to join the Watling Street at Bannaventa, the posting station near Daventry and 8 miles (13 km) from the western fringe of Northampton.

Whittlebury

Like the other former royal forests of Northamptonshire, Whittlebury Forest was the scene of bloody skirmishes between poachers and keepers. In the *Northampton Mercury* for 4th December 1749 there was a proclamation inserted on behalf of the Duke of Grafton, Chief Ranger of the forest, which details such an incident: 'Ten men, armed with Guns, Staves & by Coursing or other means, killed a Leash of Deer, one of which they carried away with them; and at the same Time attacked one of the Keepers of the said Forest, whom they beat and wounded in such a cruel Manner that they left him for dead.'

The Duke offered a 'Reward of Twenty Pounds per Man to any Person who shall discover and convict any of them'. At a time when a day's wage for a labourer was one shilling this was a large inducement but the men of the forest villages clung together in such a way that it is doubtful if there was any response.

OS 152: SP 692442. The village is on A413 4 miles (6 km) south of Towcester and there are still tracts of woodland to the west and south.

Wilbarston

Two of the oldest houses in the county are found here. In Marlow's Lane is a fifteenth-century building with its original cruck timbers and in Church Lane the Old House was formerly haunted by two ghosts — or so the story goes. These were known as Sir George and the Nun and it is said that they appeared after certain gravestones had been moved. Whatever the reason, they have not been seen since 1973, when the Bishop of Peterborough used the house as a robing room.

OS 141: SP 813884. The village is bypassed by A427 5 miles (8 km) west of Corby.

Wilby

According to a folk tale, there was a woodman at Wilby who on more than one occasion found his midday meal stolen from his bag when he left it among the trees. Soon he began to suspect a black cat of being the thief and lay in wait. From his hiding place he saw the cat delving into his bag and with a swift stroke of his axe he chopped off its paw so that it limped away, crying pitifully.

When he got home in the evening he found his wife in a sorry plight, with one of her arms only a bloody stump.

OS 152: SP 868662. Wilby is on A4500 2 miles (3 km) from the course of Wellingborough.

Woodford

One of the most bizarre relics in the county is to be found in the church of St Mary the Virgin. During restoration work to a column on the north side of the nave in 1867 the remains of a human heart were found: it can now be seen behind a glass panel in the column.

Whose heart was it? At least three suggestions have been made. A thirteenth-century burial register of Peterborough Abbey records the death of Roger de Kirkton, son-in-law to Robert Maufe of Woodford. He was buried in

(Left) The embalmed heart at Woodford and (right) the effigies of Sir Walter Trayli and his wife.

Norfolk but it is said that his embalmed heart was sent to Woodford.

At the end of the north aisle, beside the chancel, are the effigies of Sir Walter Trayli and his wife. He died in 1290 while on a crusade and another theory is that his heart was returned from there to the church of St Mary.

The most elaborate explanation is that the heart came from the body of John Styles, rector about 1550, who was expelled from his living on account of his Catholic beliefs and fled to a monastery in Belgium, taking with him a costly chalice from the church. He died soon afterwards and another priest, Andrew Powlett, brought back the chalice and Styles's heart.

Both were forgotten but in the 1860s Powlett's ghost appeared in Woodford Rectory, hovering near a panel in the wall of the hall. In a secret cavity was the chalice and a letter stating that the heart was in a pillar in the church.

OS 141: SP 969767. Woodford is just south of A604 2 miles (3 km) west of Thrapston.

Yardley Hastings

South Northamptonshire was well known for the cottage industry of making 'bone lace' and Yardley was particularly notable in the trade. Girls, sometimes as young as five years old, worked in conditions that were often crowded and squalid. To help them keep up a quick and steady rhythm with their bobbins, they were taught chants, known as 'tells'. One, known as 'The Fox', had sinister undertones:

> One lonely night, as I sat high,
> Instead of one there two passed by:
> I saw them that never saw me,
> I saw the lantern tied to the tree.
> The boughs did bend, my soul did quake,
> To see the hole that Fox did make.

This jingle was current in the 1890s in slightly varying forms in Buckinghamshire and Bedfordshire and is a rhyming version of a story usually known as *The Oxford Student.* A servant girl who had been made pregnant by her scholar lover besought him to marry her. He arranged a tryst in an apple orchard near Divinity Lane and while awaiting his coming she climbed a tree. As he approached she realised that he had a companion with him and was armed with a spade with the intention of murdering and burying her. She remained hidden in the tree and afterwards fled to her master's house and told her story. Fox, the faithless lover, was hanged.

OS 152: SP 867570. The village is astride A428 7 miles (11 km) east of Northampton.

further reading

Baker, Anne. *Glossary of Northamptonshire Words and Phrases*. Two volumes, 1864.
Baker, G. *History of Northamptonshire*. Two volumes, 1822-30.
Bridges, J. *History of Northamptonshire*. Two volumes, 1791.
Forman, Joan. *Haunted East Anglia*. Jarrold, 1990.
Harrison, Peter and May. *Spinechiller*. Sinclair, 1990.
Montagu-Douglas-Scott, Charles Henry. *Northamptonshire Songs and Others*. Three
   volumes, 1904, 1905, 1906.
Pipe, Marian. *Legends of Northamptonshire*. Spiegl Press, 1984.
— *Myths and Legends of Northamptonshire*. Spiegl Press, 1985.
— *Ghosts and Folklore of Northamptonshire*. Spiegl Press, 1986.
— *Mysteries and Memorials of Northamptonshire*. Spiegl Press, 1988.
— *Tales of Old Northamptonshire*. Spiegl Press, Countryside Books, 1990.
Sternberg, Thomas. *The Dialect and Folk-lore of Northamptonshire*. 1851, reprinted
   1971.
Story, Alfred T. *Historical Legends of Northamptonshire*. 1883.
Swift, Eric. *Folk Tales of the East Midlands*. Thomas Nelson, 1954.
Taylor, John. *Northamptonshire Witchcraft*. 1866-7.
Victoria County History of Northamptonshire. Four volumes, 1902, 1906, 1930, 1937.
Whellan, F. *History, Gazetteer and Directory of Northamptonshire*. 1849 and 1874.
Wise, Charles. *The Northamptonshire Legends*. 1905. (In verse.)

The churchyard at Welton.

Index

Page numbers in italics refer to illustrations.